SOUTH AFRICA

Dennis Kiley

SOUTH AFRICA

B. T. Batsford Ltd *London*

First published 1976

ISBN 0 7134 3252 7

Typeset by Input Typesetting Ltd., London
Printed in Great Britain by
Redwood Burn Ltd, Trowbridge & Esher
for the publishers B. T. Batsford Ltd,
4 Fitzhardinge Street, London W1H 0AH

Contents

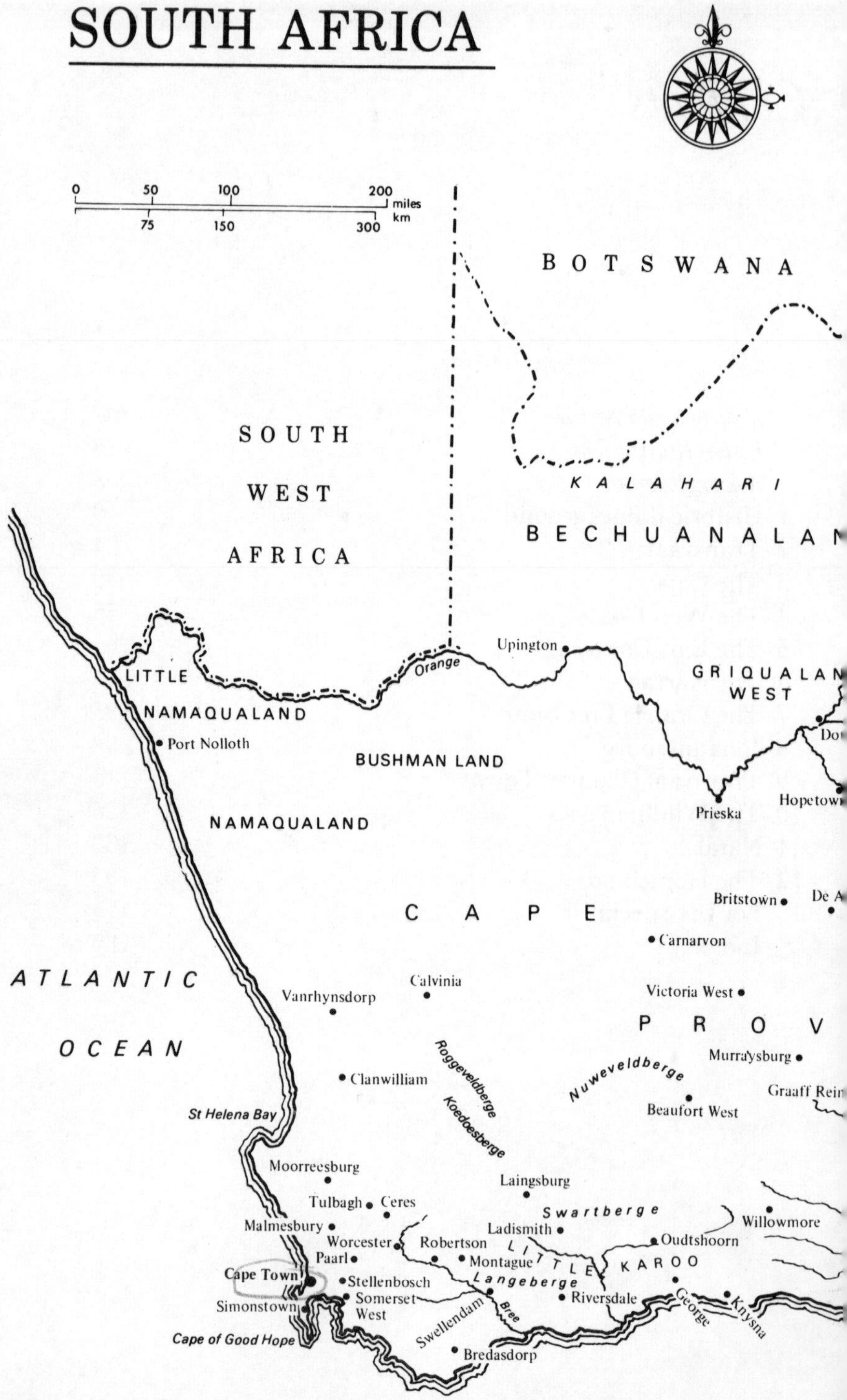
SOUTH AFRICA
0
50
100
200
miles
km
75
150
300
BOTSWANA
SOUTH
WEST
AFRICA
KALAHARI
BECHUANALAN
Upington
Orange
GRIQUALAN
WEST
Do
LITTLE
NAMAQUALAND
Port Nolloth
BUSHMAN LAND
NAMAQUALAND
Prieska
Hopetow
Britstown
De A
CAPE
Carnarvon
ATLANTIC
OCEAN
Calvinia
Vanrhynsdorp
Victoria West
PROV
Murraysburg
Roggeveldberge
Nuweveldberge
Clanwilliam
Koedoesberge
Beaufort West
Graaff Rein
St Helena Bay
Moorreesburg
Laingsburg
Tulbagh
Ceres
Swartberge
Willowmore
Malmesbury
Ladismith
Worcester
Robertson
Oudtshoorn
Paarl
Montague
LITTLE
KAROO
Cape Town
Stellenbosch
Langeberge
Simonstown
Somerset
West
Riversdale
George
Knysna
Swellendam
Bree
Cape of Good Hope
Bredasdorp

MOZAMBIQUE
Limpopo
GR
Louis Trichardt
KRUGER NATIONAL PARK
Drakensberg
Pietersburg
Potgietersrus
Olifants
Waterberge
Nylstroom
Warmbad
TRANSVAAL
Sabie
Lydenburg
Zeerust
Rustenburg
Nelspruit
Komatipoort
Crocodile
Magaliesberg
GR
Mafeking
Pretoria
Belfast
Barbeton
Witwatersrand
Middelburg
Lichtenburg
Krugersdorp
Johannesburg
Witbank
Carolina
Carletonville
Springs
Germiston
Bethal
Vereeniging
Ermelo
SWAZILAND
Klerksdorp
Harts
Vaal
Standerton
Piet Retief
Heilbron
Frankfort
Volksrust
Bloemhof
ORANGE
Vrede
Kroonstad
Vals
Christiana
Reitz
Newcastle
Paulpietersburg
Vryheid
Welkom
GR
Harrismith
Glencoe
Dundee
Senekal
Bethlehem
FREE
ZULULAND
GR
Ladysmith
Modder
Royal Natal NP
Sundays
Ficksburg
Colenso
Eshowe
Bloemfontein
Ladybrand
Estcourt
Greytown
Tugela
STATE
GR
Dewetsdorp
Caledon
Thabana Ntlenyana
NATAL
LESOTHO
Edenburg
Pietermaritzburg
Smithfield
Durban
NP
Bethulie
GRIQUALAND
Lady Grey
Aliwal North
EAST
Port Shepstone
Barkly East
Burgersdorp
PONDOLAND
Elliot
TRANSKEI
INDIAN
TEMBULAND
Umtata
Tarkastad
Queenstown
Mtn. Zebra NP
Great Kei
Cathcart
OCEAN
Bedford
Alice
Stutterheim
Adelaide
King William's Town
East London
Gt. Fish
Grahamstown
Bathurst
Port Alfred
Port Elizabeth
GR = Game Reserve NP = National Park

List of Illustrations

Acknowledgment

I should like to thank, equally, the South African Information Services and the Anti-Apartheid Movement, both of whom generously provided material. I have tried to reflect their different viewpoints. My family are to be congratulated on the patience with which they endured my efforts to settle down to work and my warm thanks are due to Barbara Hall, in whose salon I broke through from writer's block. Written sources are acknowledged in the text.

I would like to thank A. F. Kersting for illustrations 2-9, 11, 12, 22 and 23 and Satour for the remainder. The map is by Patrick Leeson.

1 Historical Background

It is not known who discovered South Africa, nor when. Certainly, it has been inhabited for a long time – for many thousands of years, of which written history only takes us back some 500. There is plenty of scattered evidence that diverse and active societies existed in different parts of the country before that, but the trail becomes harder to follow as we go further into the past, running into a maze of enigmas about a thousand years back. It is generally thought, for example, that the black African tribes were steadily moving down from the north at the time the first Westerners arrived on the scene, in the 1500's.

The Nguni group – broadly speaking, the Zulus and their linguistic relatives – show many similarities with the cattle-owning peoples in Kenya, Uganda and the Sudan in their laws and rituals, symbolism, economy, local grouping and customs such as the shaping of cattle horns. But then there are also tribal story-tellers who speak about coming from the South; it is not advisable to take too much about South Africa for granted.

Recorded history starts in recent times, with the Portuguese voyages round the Cape at the end of the 1400's. At that time, in what is now the Cape Province – which is about the size of France – there were small, lightly-built people with yellowish skins, sparse hair in 'peppercorn' tufts with features somewhere between Mongolian and Negroid, and these people were divided into two distinctive groupings which came to be known as the Hottentots and the Bushmen.

The Hottentots kept cattle and rode about on oxen. The

Bushmen were food-gatherers, hunting with great skill using poisoned arrows and sometimes creeping up on the prey disguised as animals. Several thousands of them still live in the Kalahari desert, in much the same way as they have always done, except that anthropologists may now be found creeping up to observe the Bushmen creeping up on the wildlife. They once roamed the whole of southern Africa, but they have been gradually pressed out everywhere else until only the desert is left to them. There are about 60,000 of them today in the Kalahari desert and parts of South West Africa (Namibia).

The Bushmen moved constantly in search of food, making little shelters for the night from bushes and coiling up to sleep in a small hollow scooped in the sand like a bird's nest. Their tracking is so highly developed and they can deduce so much information from a spoor that it has been known for a young Bushman to fall in love with an unknown girl just from seeing her footprints in the sand.

They sometimes put on animal skins to stalk beasts of the same species and their mimicry of animals shows a special intimacy bred from a lifetime spent among them. It has been said: 'it is not that a Bushman imitates an ostrich – he knows exactly what it feels like to be an ostrich.' They perform dances in which individuals take the part of certain animals, and the dance may go on all night in the event of a great celebration such as the killing of an eland. The effect can be very hypnotic and people from other tribes who have attended such dances will often tell you, with complete conviction, that the Bushmen, on those occasions, 'turn into lions and hyenas and other animals', and in Botswana where most of them live, a certain mystical fear surrounds them for this reason. In their myths, passed on by word of mouth, they speak of a time when animals spoke like men, and there was friendship between them.

The Hottentot cattle herders were an adaptable people and receptive to new ideas and technologies. They linked up physically with the white newcomers who began to arrive systematically after Jan van Riebeek set up his refreshment station for the Dutch East India ships at Cape Town in 1652.

It must have been about nine months after the first White sailor set foot in South Africa that the first member of a new South African nation was born – the so-called 'Cape Coloureds'.

This new group was added to later by other newcomers, such as Malay slaves from Batavia and black Africans from the North, while white immigrants continued to arrive and mingle with the inhabitants over the centuries. In the early days the first white settlers were paid a bounty of ten Dutch guilders by the Dutch East India Company if they would marry a Hottentot woman, since it was felt this would encourage them to settle permanently and provide the necessary farm produce for ships trading between Europe and the East. Later arrivals, higher up the social scale, frowned on such unions in accordance with the social values of their times. But sexual mixing continued although formal intermarriage was fairly rare, and it was only well into the present century that sexual intercourse between the races was made illegal.

For 'Bushman' and 'Hottentot' some authorities prefer the names 'San' and 'Khoi-Khoi'.

The life-styles and languages of these two peoples are so dissimilar that they have generally been regarded as two separate races, but if you ask South Africans in the Cape to describe the racial characteristics of these people you will get conflicting and confusing reports. The reason for this is that they are in fact from the same racial stock, though differing greatly in their languages and way of life.

At the time of van Riebeek's arrival, the Hottentots were well off for cattle and sheep – about six head of cattle per person was common. They killed them on ritual occasions and hunted, fished and collected honey and wild plants for food. Like the Bushmen, they carried knapsacks on their backs – unlike the black Bantu races, who carried things balanced on their heads, and still do. They made their clothes from the skins of sheep, oxen and such wild animals as seals, wild-cats and jackals. Really important people wore badger or otter-skin garments. Their humped cattle were the ancestors of the present well-known Afrikander cattle, and they trained them to a high level. They could call them by whistling and they rode them and used pack-oxen.

As white settlers multiplied, the Hottentots came under more and more pressure for grazing land. Groups of them wandered many hundreds of miles away and some of their descendants are still living in 'bastard' colonies on the Orange River and in the far Nort-West Cape and South West Africa. There is a famous one at Rehoboth which had its own postage stamps until very recently. There was trouble with the newcomers about the grazing land right from the start, and the first serious fight over it was in 1659, when the 'Capemen' Hottentots tried to expel the Dutch for taking pasture land in what is now a suburb of Cape Town known as Rosebank.

From about 1680 the Dutch were establishing a form of indirect rule over the Hottentots, at first by mediating in their disputes. There was a good deal of mingling between them, it helped trade and the security of the settlers if the Dutch East India Company had some formal power over the Hottentots, and by the 1680's the Company was presenting copper-headed staffs with its own mark to the chiefs of Hottentot hordes whom it recognized. As the Hottentots gradually lost their own land and herds they stayed on among the Dutch as servants and herders.

It was not, however, a one-way traffic and in the early centuries a way of life common to Whites as well as Hottentots evolved in many of the outlying districts, with the settlers learning much about animals and grazing lands from the herders and hunters they were displacing and coming to dominate.

But the Whites had a continuing link with a literate and rapidly-developing culture overseas, particularly through the Christian religion, and this gave them a permanent advantage insofar as their relations with the other groups were competitive.

The Hottentots' language gave way gradually to a form of kitchen Dutch, which they and the white colonists together developed into Afrikaans, a new indigenous language with a lively idiom of its own. Those of their descendants who are still visibly people of colour are now known as 'Coloureds', and those who are not have merged into the white race of South Africa.

Racial difference, and colour in particular, has been a highly controversial issue in South Africa over the years. Leaving aside the political and moral questions raised, (about which the South African newspapers, among other commentators, write volumes every day), newcomers to the country are often confused and embarrassed to find that some people whom they think are obviously Coloured are in fact officially White, whereas others who appear obviously White are officially Coloured.

At one stage, official efforts were made to classify these South Africans on the racial borderlines, and a Race Classification Tribunal was set up to take decisions about individual cases. Some of the results were tragic, with 'White' children disowning brothers and sisters who were classified 'Coloured'.

Under increasing pressure from the outside world, racial discrimination is being progressively abandoned in South Africa and although there is still a weird collection of racial laws on the statute books, newcomers will generally steer clear of trouble if they approach people without discrimination. If you happen to hold and voice very strong views about race, either for or against racial discrimination, you will almost certainly cause serious offence to somebody present. Again, things are not what they seem on the surface and some Afrikaners are passionate liberals, some English-speaking South Africans are passionately right-wing, some black South Africans believe in 'separate development', and others hate it.

The Bushmen did not participate much in this creation of a new people. Their habits of hunting their food made them the natural enemies of pastoral people of whatever origin, and with the coming of firearms they were increasingly hunted down.

It was the Bushmen who produced the first recorded history of South Africa in the form of their rock paintings, though it has not proved possible to date them. These paintings bear a fascinating resemblance to the rock paintings found in Spanish caves, many of them are of great vigour and beauty, and they are to be found all over South Africa and South West Africa. They are well worth a visit (local guide-books will point out the way) and nowadays they are often carefully preserved and protected. One of the paintings of the latest period in the Drakensberg mountains of Natal, shows white-skinned men arriving on horseback wearing hats and carrying guns. Significantly after that the rock paintings cease.

In what are now the provinces of Natal, the Orange Free State and the Transvaal, the dominant people for some thousands of years appear to have been black Africans of various tribes. They were also cattle herders and cultivators and were technologically well ahead of the Hottentots, with their agriculture and ability to smelt and work iron. At the time of their first contact with the West, they had developed fairly extensive and complex systems of administration and the accounts of early travellers produce a picture of a society which must have been, on the whole, comfortable and well-ordered.

The discovery of Chinese pottery and other items in archaeological sites many hundreds of miles inland, suggests some tenuous trade contact between South Africa and the Indian Ocean countries, dating back about 1500 years. Such valuables as copper and gold, as well as traditional African exotica like *karosses* made of the skins of rare animals, have been coming out of the hinterland of southern Africa for at least 1000 years, with imported luxuries and fine artwork like celadon-ware from China finding their way to remote tribal uplands in exchange. So the pattern of primary products being used to pay for high-grade imported manufactured goods is not exactly new in South Africa.

Arab traders have been active on the coast of East Africa as far south as present-day Tanzania for at least 1000 years. Before that, there is a report of a Phoenician crew sent by the Pharaoh Neche making a voyage of exploration round Africa, going down the Eastern coastline and coming back into the Mediterranean 'past the pillars of Hercules'.

Herodotus mentions an attempt by one Sataspes to sail round Africa. He went down the west coast, apparently, and after many months of following it south he reached a point where the inhabitants were pygmies, 'wearing clothes of palm trees'.

That suggests he must have reached as far south as the Congo river, unless in those times pygmies were found further up the west coast of Africa than the Congo basin.

But 'real' contact on a continuing basis was made between Europe and South Africa in the course of the Portuguese opening up a sea route to the Indies, notably Calicut, the great spice centre.

The story of how the Portuguese opened up that sea-route is one of the great sagas of human achievement. Their motives were solidly practical for they saw that the route was 'vital to their commercial, territorial and missionary ambitions'. The bravery and enterprise, the years of scientific preparation which went into the first voyages of exploration were epic in their proportions. Navigational systems and ship design had to be improved and they then had to venture far out into the Atlantic before they found the winds that could take them reliably south. As Christopher Bell points out: '. . . a caravel, the sort of ship in which the Portuguese undertook these expeditions into unknown waters, tiny cockleshells of 50 tons or thereabouts, could be handled by three men and two boys and, even when fully manned, often carried a crew of less than 30'.

By 1482 Diogo Cao reached the Congo River and sent his ambassadors inland into the forest to contact the ruler, the Manicongo. He left them there while he tried to push on further and it was three years before he saw them again. But these voyages and adventures were building up knowledge and experience for the final breakthrough – the rounding of Africa and opening up of a route to the Indian Ocean, which Bartolemu Dias was to achieve a few years later, in 1488.

King Joao provided Bartolemu Dias with two caravels and a store-ship. The king, like his great-uncle, Henry the Navigator, 'had technical advisers, mathematicians, astronomers, cartographers, and shipwrights, who considered how every difficulty that Cao had reported might be overcome' (Christopher Bell).

They took with them several African men and women who had learnt Portuguese and experienced Portuguese culture, and put them ashore at various points to make contact with the local people and report back to Dias on his return journey. Alas, nothing is known of the fate of these emissaries.

Pushing on south, Dias left his store-ship in a hospitable bay, either in South-West Africa or Angola – it is not known which. The men on the store-ship they left behind, (if it was indeed in South-West Africa and not further north) would very likely have seen the elusive Bushmen, 'short and sparse in form, tawny coloured, the men armed with bows and poisoned arrows.'

If there were Hottentot villages nearby they would have been living, in that area, in conical structures of poles almost like wigwams, which were covered with bullock hides. They kept cattle and sheep, but lived very largely off the sea, and 'with their 16-foot lances they could spear seven or ten-pound fishes at a distance of 30 yards and arrows shot from their longbows could drop a gull on the wing at a distance of 50 yards.'

They had a technique of drying and preserving seabirds so that their flesh lost all taste of fish and could be kept for a whole year. Dias may well have bartered with them for such dried birds for his crew to eat. The Hottentots of that region were still living in much the same way until the 1880's.

It is a wild, desolate, sandy shore for many hundreds of miles, much of it the forbidding 'Skeleton Coast' where the surf breaks on shoals for six miles out to sea, protecting the world's greatest deposits of gem diamonds in the desert sands of the Namib.

But there are a few bays and inlets. If it was Walvis Bay where Dias left his store-ship, then the scenery which he and his men saw would have been the same as that described by James Alexander in 1837, and indeed it is still very little altered to this day.

1 The Big Hole, Kimberley
2 In the Bantu kraal in Transvaal

> There is a broad sandy beach round the bay, and sand-hills heaped up in various forms inland, and the general look of things here is very wild and Arabian-like. The quantities of sea fowl we saw on the shores of the bay, winging their way, and screaming over its green waters, were immense.
>
> Pelicans with snow-white plumage, and a light blush of red on the wings, appeared in vast flocks; flamingoes with outstretched necks and drooping bills stalked along the beach, and allowed us to approach them; wild geese in long strings flew overhead . . . and sand-larks . . . hurried along the wet sand before us.

But that sandy shore, swept by the icy Benguela current, presents a very different picture to the point where Dias was to make his next landfall, having at last rounded the Cape. He sailed out of the bay in his two tiny vessels, into the uncharted South Atlantic. For five days they beat against southerly winds then turned away from Africa, south-west into the open ocean, looking for the winds which might or might not exist to blow them back to Africa. They struggled on and on through variable winds, until they appear to have hit the 'roaring forties', which ocean liners will not venture into today if they can help it.

These winds blow – indeed, they roar and scream – round the world. It was exactly what they needed. After many more days of no doubt hectic sailing they calculated that they were by now long past the point at which they should have once again found the west coast of Africa.

They were right – they had sailed right past the bottom point of the great continent, much too far out to sea to see it.

Eventually, turning north, they made their landfall in what is now called Mossel Bay – nearly 200 miles east of Cape Town – lying on the temperate east coast of South Africa where the landscape is green, with grass, bushes and dense forests in the mountains behind. 'In the open places beyond the sandy shore, herds of humped cattle grazed, watched by small men with tightly-curled hair.'

They marvelled at the size and quality of the cattle, but

3 A Bantu woodcarver in the Transvaal

were not at first able to make any friendly contact with the herdsmen. But Europe had 'discovered' South Africa and from this time on, South Africa began supplying passing ships on a regular basis. In the 1500's Portuguese ships called in regularly, and to this day a 'post office tree' may be seen on a hill overlooking the sea in Mossel Bay where they left messages for each other.

They picked up fresh food and water at the Cape itself and at points such as Mossel Bay and Algoa Bay, now Port Elizabeth, some 700 miles further up the coast from the Cape Peninsula.

The earliest records of any intimate contact between overseas races and South Africans were made by shipwrecked sailors and tribesmen. Among the black tribes, such survivors seem generally to have been treated hospitably, provided that they followed the age-old stranger's rule for survival – excite neither fear nor envy.

What is perhaps most interesting about the comments of Western travellers in South Africa in the 1500's and 1600's, is the level of comfort, prosperity and the generally civilized manner of living which they encountered. The vulgar picture of 'savages living in mud huts' which served many uniformed westerners as an image of Africa gives no clue to the extent of the society which black indigenous South Africans had built up at the time of their first contacts with the White newcomers from over the sea.

Some of the most interesting accounts of life in South Africa, from a foreigner's point of view, come from the survivors of shipwrecks from the 1500's on. They were often well treated by the inhabitants and settled among them. Several of them comment on the way in which the inhabitants travelled about the country by running. A Portuguese writer shipwrecked in the Santo Alberto in 1593 says: 'they are shod with two or three soles of raw leather fastened together in a round shape, and secured to the feet with straps; in these they run with great lightness.'

The journalist on the *Nossa Senhora de Belem,* which went aground in Xhosa territory in 1635, is even more impressed, and says: 'The men of this country are very lean and upright, tall of stature, and handsome. They can endure great labour, hunger and cold; they live 200 years and even more in good health, and with all their teeth. They are so light that they can run over the rugged mountains as fleetly as stags.'

Indeed, to this day you may meet a party of young tribesmen, particularly in the Transkei, loping along over the hills for mile after mile at a sort of comfortable gliding trot, carrying their fighting-sticks and probably looking very much the same as their fleet-footed ancestors of 1635.

The survivors of the *Stavenisse,* wrecked in 1686, who lived among the Xhosa for three years, reported in great detail on the rule of law which prevailed among them, and on their hospitality. Chillingly, in the light of what was to come later, they also reported that slavery was unknown among these people: 'It would be impossible to buy any slaves there, for they would not part with their children, or any of their connections for anything in the world, loving one another with a most remarkable strength of affection.'

Slavery does not appear to have been known among the Xhosa and Zulus, although practised on their northern borders and there is only one recorded report of Zulus dealing in slaves by a Captain Robert Drury, who bought 74 boys and girls from them in 1719 at the Bay of Natal.

The *Stavenisse* party and others after them found that in the Bantu-speaking societies disputes were settled in court, trade was regulated, and the chiefs themselves were answerable to their own privy councils, which could try them and fine them for transgressions.

In the absence of writing, the 'literature' was verbal, and story-tellers were important figures taking great pride in their art. Intricate legal cases decided by tribal courts were one source of inspiration for traditional tales, told with great verve and panache by African bards and handed down verbatim from one generation of story-tellers to the next. Famous love-affairs, the deeds of great warriers, the supernatural, all provided their crop of tales, as in the West.

Such traditions have left a considerable imprint. Anybody

who has spent time in the company of black South Africans will have experienced their talent for oratory, mimicry and the relish and minutely-observed detail with which they will tell a story. In the 'shebeens' (African drinking clubs) of Johannesburg one of the favourite impromptu entertainments is to re-enact some encounter which happened during the working day.

It is a very amusing and ironic commentary on the South African way of life, but very few white South Africans can have seen it, because of the social gulf dividing them from Africans. Many of them would be astounded to see how that meek, submissive 'office boy' takes them off, to the hilarity of his mates, and what a wealth of detailed information about their business and private lives he usually throws in for good measure.

In the 1960's when black actors and singers from South Africa first started appearing in musicals and plays about their own country on the stages of London's West End, London critics confessed themselves staggered by the high level of their acting ability, understandable when one considers that acting is part of their culture.

Their striking sociability has not changed much since a writer in 1686 described it thus: 'In their intercourse with each other, they are very civil, polite and talkative, saluting each other, whether male or female, young or old, whenever they meet; asking whence they come, and whither they are going, what is their news, and whether they have learned any new dances or tunes . . .'

Of course, one must not get too sentimental imagining a vanished golden age for South African black people. There was an unpleasant side to their society as well, with much evidence of witchcraft, superstition and cruelty – again, inviting interesting parallels with Europe of the same time. Generally though, they enjoyed a peaceful society until the rise of the Zulu warlords spread a wave of violence in the early nineteenth century, and increasing white pressure began to force them into a new way of life.

However, after the opening of the Cape route by the

Portuguese, the most critical event in the country's history was when the Dutch East India Company set up a trading post at Cape Town in 1652. From this moment, and at an ever-increasing pace, the country became really involved in the world import-export trade, starting off with South Africa supplying vegetables and meat and the outside world supplying in exchange luxuries and equipment such as iron ploughs, guns and textiles.

2 Transvaal

Brightly-coloured giant parasols by the side of the road, behind them an expanse of arid yellow-and-red veld. Under the parasols, large tables and chairs, one young couple having coffee with another. A picnic? No – property speculators at work.

You are looking at the Transvaal. The young couple who have set up the impromptu roadside estate office are trying to sell a building plot on a potential township. They do it every week-end – during the week they are both busy at their jobs. They are trying to get rich as quickly as possible. It is the Transvaal game.

The excitement of big money made quickly hangs in the dry crisp air. The sun is fierce, blazing down almost every day of the year. The white people here have keen eyes, sharp voices, ready to jump at a good chance, driving their cars very fast and themselves very hard. The black peoples' eyes are more guarded, as if watching and waiting for their own chance. The atmosphere is edgy, tense, exciting, dangerous.

It was all built on gold, found and exploited almost overnight. The spirit of the gold rush still hangs in the air. The brittle, eye-narrowing climate helps.

The blacks were here farming, smelting iron and mining copper long before the whites came on the scene. The farming and hunting Boers were the first to arrive, sparring their way cautiously in among the tribesmen, conducting a sort of dialogue with them, bargaining, sometimes fighting, about grazing rights, later persuading and cajoling some of the blacks to work for them.

When the gold was found in the 1880's, white people poured in and it was every man for himself and the weakest to the wall.

The blacks were largely elbowed aside in the grabbing and snatching for wealth. But they were always there, in among the whites, working side by side with them, still owning herds of cattle and even their own farms until very recent times.

It is very difficult to get a clear and unbiased picture of the development of the two races together in the Transvaal. The official picture is outrageously bowdlerised and cleaned up – just as misleading as the picture viewed from the opposite direction, that of the extreme left and underground opposition groups. Somewhere in between the wildly conflicting accounts lies the truth. The Whites were not all rapacious gold-hunters. The Blacks were not all gentle-eyed, exploited herdsmen. There has always been much dialogue between them, much vigorous interaction, both have benefitted more from each other than either likes to admit.

The great South African writer Hermann Bosman tells the story of Boer and African elders following a long exhausting battle. After they had agreed on the terms of peace, sitting round and talking together at great length, they exchanged gifts as a mark of friendship. The Boers were rather puzzled that among the gifts which the Africans gave them was one which they seemed to regard as the most important, although it seemed to the Boers to have no value. It was just a clay pot filled with earth. But after thinking about it its true significance dawned on them and they accepted it with appropriate grace – they, who were also farmers.

The land is more than valuable to any farming nation, it is sacred, and as times change and land has to be divided up in different ways, it excites strong emotions anywhere in the world. More so if a conquering, invading race appears to have seized most of the best land for itself.

White South Africans in general, and particularly those in the Transvaal, have a bad conscience about land ownership. If questioned too closely about this many of them will fly into a rage. There is an enormous apparatus of laws and regulations having the general effect of preventing Africans and other 'Non-Europeans' from owning or occupying land in so-called White areas. The arguments about it have been repeated interminably, and there is no need to bore ourselves by going over them yet again. But there are some more interesting aspects worth considering.

One is that some genuine regional development and decentralisation of growth centres is achieved under the general umbrella of this 'separate development' policy.

Most countries have similar problems of cities growing too fast and too big and most of the developed ones have formulated various policies to try and counteract the excessive gravitational attraction of the big centres. The British Government, for example, offers all manner of incentives to industrialists to push their new developments ahead in the comparatively 'underdeveloped' areas of Wales and Scotland rather than in the over-industrialized Midlands or the over-populated South-East.

Whether it is right or wrong for a government to hold the power to force whole groups of the population to live in one part of the country and prevent them living in another is an argument outside the scope of this book, but having such power certainly enables a government to make some large-scale plans. However, social and economic forces in South Africa work against the official segregation policy. At businessmen's conferences in the Transvaal, for example, one hears factory-owners usingan extraordinary expression about 'trying to squeeze Bantu out of the department' a highly cartoonable concept.

It refers to the regulations restricting the ratio of black to white workers to about three black to one white in most of the Witwatersrand industrial area, part of the policy of strictly keeping down the numbers of Africans allowed in 'White' areas.

It has some strange results. I have been in a factory where most of the work was done at the dead of night, with air-raid type blinds drawn and noise kept to a minimum, because the owner was illegally employing far more Africans than he would have been able to 'squeeze out of the Department' legally. At another factory, two miles away, the owner employed a ratio of more than 50 black to one white and simply ignored the law: 'a little present here and there'. he waggled his flat hand expressively.

This kind of bribery is more widespread in South Africa than in most of Western Europe, but far less tolerated than in most of the rest of Africa. By international standards there is not much petty corruption, though from time to time there are spectacular examples of corruption in very high places. Again, it is not always tolerated, the government is run mostly by Afrikaners, and Afrikaners have a very strong puritanical streak deriving from their Dutch Reformed religion. For example, in Pretoria recently I came upon a case where three Afrikaners – they happened to be politicians – applied to another Afrikaner whom they thought would help them with a lucrative but illegal currency operation they had planned. Instead he gave them a furious dressing-down and threatened them with arrest if they tried it on again.

The point of this little example is just that no one group has a monopoly on corruption or uprightness in South Africa, though members of one group will frequently point to another and say: 'there're the ones behind it all'.

The main racial groups are generally suspicious of each other, though to say so openly in South Africa is a heresy and much pious nonsense is talked on the subject. There are an immense welter of Parliamentary Acts, other regulations and customs designed to keep the groups as separate as possible, and there is also an Act – the 'Incitement Act' – threatening dire penalties for anyone who tries to exacerbate the situation by inciting members of one race to hatred against another. It is probably very necessary.

Africans, by and large, dislike Afrikaners, whom they regard as officious bullies. But again, there are a great many exceptions to the generalisation and you will find Africans who have spent their whole lives very happily living with Afrikaans families, and Afrikaners who devote their lives to working among Africans. The relationship is generally paternalistic, with all the good and bad that that entails. Those Africans and Afrikaners who have developed a personal realtionship within this system often get on well enough together, and of course much mutual regard and even affection is possible under paternalism, and the national mythology is full of stories of mutual help and indeed heroism and self-sacrifice which members of those two groups have shown for each other over the centuries – as well as of fighting, treachery and savage deeds on both sides.

In a way, the Afrikaners and the Africans are the two groups who have the most intimate relationship in the whole country, constantly aware of each other, working together, warily sparring and feinting and feeling for a weakness in the other's position, occasionally striking out, sometimes – another great heresy – even embracing (illegally, according to the Immorality Act.)

I once asked Chief Luthuli, the African nationalist leader who won the Nobel Peace Prize towards the end of his life, what he thought would happen if there was a general breakdown of law and order and the white authorities had to ask men like himself to sit down with them and try to work out a solution. (It was at an extremely threatening time in the country's history, just before the shootings at Sharpville when there had been many serious riots, and it seemed as if the country trembled on the brink of some kind of popular revolution.) He replied: 'I think if it really came to that we would manage it vey well between us. We understand those people (the Afrikaners) very well, and they also understand us.' He chuckled and added: 'as a matter of fact, if you look at the figures for prosecutions, and the names involved, you will see that they even like us physically.' (A large majority of the white men prosecuted under the Immorality Act were Afrikaners.)

The Afrikaner's main ancestors are not the Dutch as is generally thought. The Dutch played a critical role in establishing a settlement at the Cape, but they did not continue to settle in the country in any great numbers, and Afrikaans ancestry has considerably more German in it than

Dutch, and indeed, more French as well. Recent studies give the ethnic origin of the Afrikaners as 45 percent German, 27 percent French, 22 percent Dutch and 6 percent 'the rest'. Many of them are large and blonde, as might be expected, but many, too, are small and dark and would look much more at home in a French village than a German one.

Their closest relatives are the Cape Coloured people, who grew up from the steady mingling of indigenous white stock and indigenous black races, mainly Hottentot but with admixtures of Malay and African.

Again, much nonsense is talked in official South African text-books about the origins of the Cape Coloured people, and it is suggested that they were the result of 'miscegenation between indigenous races and imported slaves,' and the like. This is, of course, part of the story – though the word 'miscegenation' is a sinister one heavily loaded with overtones of disapproval. There is a voluminous documentation on the subject, but even without that, common-sense is enough to show that white people are hardly likely to have been living in conditions of considerable intimacy among black people for nearly 500 years without some, at least, of them, producing racially-mixed babies.

The Coloured people live mainly in the Cape, where most of them originated. The Cape is immensely racially-conscious, though traditionally much more tolerant and liberal than the Transvaal.

Generally speaking in the Free State, Natal or Transvaal, people are black or white and there is no great consciousness of the in-betweens. In the Cape, the in-betweens themselves are carefully graded, and so caught up in the whole process have the Coloured people themselves become that groups of them have been known to arrange social functions for 'slightly coloured' people only, rejecting those of too dark a shade.

'Coloured' people of mixed blood are of course found throughout South Africa, but their heartland is the Western Cape Province, where about two million of them live. Culturally they are almost identical to White South Africans: their home language is either Afrikaans or English (more often

Afrikaans), they wear western clothes and eat the South African variants of western food, with some excellent spicy dishes of their own inherited from Malay ancestors. Some of them are Muslims – the most important difference from the White communities.

In general, their tastes, values, ambitions are all much the same as those of the White people among whom they live.

They came to be gradually integrated with the White community in the Cape, living in the same suburbs, sitting on the City Council, and having at least one major White school open to them (South African College, Cape Town) for many years. After 1948 they were subjected to a programme of racial discrimination, being moved out of White suburbs into areas specially zoned for them, deprived of their parliamentary vote and generally harried by the Government. At the same time, however, the country's rapid post-war growth was creating more and more jobs for their well-developed skills – the Government wanted to kick them out, the economy wanted to suck them in, so to speak. In the event, economic rationality has in general been prevailing and Coloured people are well distributed in all occupations in the Cape, though generally at lower levels than the White population.

They are a witty, Cockney people, liable to be exceedingly sharp-tongued in argument. They have been mistreated and they are well aware of it and there is no need for any stranger to be taken in by official pronouncements on the joys of separate development for Coloureds – they have hundreds of articulate spokesmen who are frequently on record attacking it, and in conversation they will state their case bluntly enough if asked, though like all South Africans, they will show some fear of the ubiquitous Special Branch when first speaking to strangers.

In South African liberal mythology the Special Branch are blamed for a great deal of official intimidation, but in fact they seem to have acquired a bogey-man image in excess of their actual deeds, considerable though these have been.

There is in South Africa a sort of creeping authoritarianism which is all-pervasive and achieves a much greater limitation on freedom of speech and association than the much-dreaded Special Branch would be able to do, or indeed would probably wish to do anyway. Businessmen talking to strangers discussing some aspect of official policy they find absurd, may lower their voices, look around uneasily, and say: 'I'd better not say too much.' If you press them and ask what they are so nervous of it emerges that they are not frightened of being dragged off in the night by the Special Branch for speaking out against Government policy – it isn't that bad – but they have a generalized feeling that 'if you say too much against them they can make things very awkward for you.' They will mumble on uneasily about licences, permits and so on if pressed further.

Formally, there is considerable freedom of speech in South Africa, more so than in most of the independent countries of black Africa, but there is a formidable apparatus of laws which obliges the Press to censor itself – The Supression of Communism Act, the Incitement Act, the Prisons Act, and many others.

Nevertheless, any South African journalist who can find his way through the maze of legislation affecting him can speak up and attack the Government and its policies and as long as he keeps within the law he will probably not suffer any official harrassment. The opposition Press, therefore, remains outspokenly critical.

But at a more diffuse general level, there is a subservience to the wishes of authority not generally found in Western countries. The official attitudes about the place of authority are Victorian-Germanic. Schoolchildren are there to learn, not to annoy their teachers by asking questions, and certainly not by answering back or arguing.

The Afrikaners, in particular, have great reverence for teachers, elders and all persons in positions of authority. Their university professors are appalled at the suggestion that in overseas universities the students are encouraged, at seminars, to challenge the views and theories of their elders and betters.

At an educational level the effects are both good and bad. There is a tradition of extremely hard work, thoroughness and attention to quality which has earned South Africa an international reputation in several fields – dental work, general medical care, mining engineering, nature conservation, to mention only a few. But Western educationists find South African students, particularly those from Afrikaans universities, in general unable to think critically or cope adaptively with unexpected new situations. The degrees which they have laboured so hard to earn, particularly in arts faculties, are not always acceptable in European universities.

Many Coloured people still live and work on wine farms, where they are paid part of their wages in cheap, new wine of an abominable quality (if you doubt that, try a bottle). The general ration is about three bottles a day, most of them are chronic alcoholics from their teens until their death at a very early age from the combined effects of malnutrition and alcoholism. Wine farmers are caught up in the system and will often say: 'We don't like it at all, but if you won't give them wine you can't get any workers.' Some of them do manage to break the vicious spiral and develop a non-alcoholic work-force with a better standard of living, but it is a sad aspect of the otherwise beautiful wine farms of the Cape.

Many of the Coloureds are fishermen, and they have a long tradition of craftsmanship, particularly among the Cape Malays, a distinctive Muslim community within the Coloured population descended from the Malay slaves.

In spite of their various political and economic disabilities, they are in general a very jolly people, gregarious, noisy, fond of parties, drinking and singing. One of the country's leading Afrikaans writers, Uys Krige, has written a most moving and beautiful extended poem about them called 'Die Ballade van die Groot Begeerte' (The Ballad of the Great Longing) in which he celebrates the nostalgia evoked by a Cape Coloured soldier in World War Two, far from home, strumming his guitar and singing to himself.

The English-speaking people of South Africa are, in general, the urban sector, though here again there are many exceptions and you can meet rugby-playing Afrikaans-speaking farmers with names like Hamish MacGregor.

The English began to arrive as immigrants in South Africa after 1820 and have played a very important part in the history of the country, bringing with them various British traditions of commerce, education, a free press and a whole host of attitudes and traditions which have been absorbed into the South African way of life.

The surprise for the newcomer and perhaps even for the South African who stops to think about it, is that they have remained so distant from the Afrikaners, while living among them so intimately. There are of course numerous intermarriages, friendships and business relationships between the two groups, but on the whole they are two quite distinct cultures and regard each other with a certain wariness and, in certain cases unfortunately, even suspicion and hostility.

At worst, the Afrikaner tends to look upon the English-speaking white South African as an untrustworthy city slicker of shallow moral values. Similarly, those English-speaking South Africans who dislike Afrikaners tend to regard them as crude, narrow-minded and bigoted and invent numerous insulting nicknames for them, calling them 'Hairybacks', 'Rock spiders', 'Jaaps', 'Skaaps' (Sheep), and even, in Rhodesia, 'Ropes' ('because they are thick, hairy and twisted'.)

The country is full of 'Van der Merwe' stories about an Afrikaans rustic of legendary stupidity. But they are generally quite good-natured – mocking, but not vicious.

On the other side of the coin, one finds much admiration for the toughness and honesty of the Afrikaner among English-speaking South Africans, and you hear many tales of their hospitality and generosity – and will experience both if you get to know any Afrikaners at all well.

Among Afrikaners there is a certain admiration for the urban skills of the 'Englishman' and for his links with a great culture. Many of the older Afrikaners are unashamed Anglophiles, educated by English schoolteachers, and cherishing a knowledge of English literature.

The rural-urban distinction between the two groups is in

any case rapidly breaking down, with hundreds of thousands of Afrikaners permanently urban people. Both White groups tend to be fond of the land and to be proud of links with farming relatives or friends, or to try and run smallholdings or 'plots' as they are called locally, where they do a little farming themselves as a hobby.

Afrikaners tend to take criticism of themselves or their country badly, particularly from 'outsiders' but also from people they know well. They will often say: 'We don't mind criticism, as long as it's constructive,' and then proceed to become very hurt and defensive when one offers constructive criticism. This perhpas reflects their general attitude of intense seriousness and commitment. If a particular South African achievement is praised they take it personally, they glow. If it is decried, it affects them equally personally and they find it difficult to take an objective stand and are hurt. They take friendship very seriously; they will expect new friends to 'drop in' and visit them at any odd times, unannounced and uninvited, preferably bringing their wife and children with them, and then they will press the visitors to stay for a meal. Naturally, they expect this to be reciprocal; they will go to great lengths and make considerable sacrifices to help their friends and even much more, their relations. They attach so much importance to being in complete harmony with their friends that one family I knew who had gone on holiday each year with another family in identical station-wagons, nearly broke up the whole friendship because one of the families eventually insisted on changing to a different type of car. To an unsympathetic outsider such things may sound trivial or small-minded, but they proceed from a different cultural concept of human relationships and if you want to get on with Afrikaners it is worth studying them.

Their frequently large and rugged appearance is also misleading: they have a certain delicacy of manners which is liable to be misunderstood as 'touchiness'. Among men bad language is much less usual than among British people of the same sort of background. Presumably because of their strict Calvinistic background, they are likely to find it distasteful

4 Chapman's Peak Drive, near Cape Town

and a gigantic Afrikaans rugby-player of gnarled and ferocious aspect is likely to wince at English rugby-songs.

The Coloured people, by contrast, habitually use a rich and varied flow of bad language in Afrikaans (though this tends to fade out higher up the social scale) and the flow of obscene insults to be heard from a pair of quarrelling fishermen on a Saturday night can be little masterpieces of invective, sheer folk art. Unfortunately, they are unprintable in this context, and in any case they should be heard in Afrikaans to be fully savoured.

There is also a considerable Indian population, and they tend to be generally smallish traders, although in recent years some of them have become very considerable business figures indeed. They too, suffer from ambivalent attitudes among the other racial groups. They tend to work very long hours in their shops, and to enjoy themselves on their days off by piling a large family into the biggest and shiniest motor-car they can buy, and driving about.

In a car-worshipping society this type of visible demonstration of apparent affluence excites much envy from Whites with smaller cars, and much invidious comment. There is a certain grudging admiration for their industry, but they are victims of one of the many cherished fallacies in South African economic folk-lore, to the effect that 'a middle-man does nothing, produces nothing, just makes money out of buying and selling.' How the distributive system would work in the absence of such 'parasitic middlemen' is not usually discussed.

Apart from their big motor-cars, Indians tend to keep a low profile and get on with their own lives. They have been harried, like the Cape Coloureds, on racial grounds and their livelihood has been attacked by forcing them out of the trading neighbourhoods where they have been established for generations. But at the same time, to be fair to the authorities, they have been given some separate facilities such as an Indian University in Durban which is said to be well-equipped and of a good standard, and separate residential areas, some of which have been very attractively developed.

5 Looking over Cape Town from the lower slopes of Table Mountain

Most of the people in South Africa, of course, are Africans. In round figures, the total population is 25 million, of whom 18 million are African, four million White, two million Coloured and 700,000 Asian.

The Zulus alone (4,026,000) almost equal the Whites (4,200,000) and so do the Xhosa, (3,930,000) of the same language group. Then come eight nations or language-groups – in descending numerical order: Tswana, Sepedi (North Sotho), Seshoeshoe (South Sotho), Shangaan, Swazi, Venda, South Ndebele and North Ndebele. The Africans have ten of their own languages. Most of them speak their own language and can make their way in one of the two official White languages, but in big cities like Johannesburg they are usually familiar with at least four languages.

The White authorities are enthusiastic about the tribal differences between the various African groups and try to foster their development in separate ethnic groups as far as possible. Politically aware Africans are less enthusiastic.

The greatest concentrations of Africans live in the vicinity of Johannesburg and its associated Reef towns, which stretch for nearly 100 miles along the line of the gold reef. To the eye of the newcomer, and indeed the Whites who live surrounded by them, they live a curious semi-visible existence in which they can be seen every day in their tens of thousands in the streets of Johannesburg, in the offices, homes and factories, apparently mixing with White people, but their social and family life is conducted elsewhere – from ten to 20 miles away, in huge black suburbs or locations, where they live a busy and often extremely stressful life, in areas which Whites may visit only with special permits and between strictly limited daylight hours.

In these areas the social vitality is enormous, partly because of the dense concentration of people living closely together, probably also because of certain sociable, extrovert qualities in the African's own culture, whatever his tribe. They organise themselves into hundreds of clubs – social, sporting, drinking, debating, singing – and thousands of religious sects. They live in semi-western style, mostly in small houses, though with very limited services – no electricity, no waterborne sewage system, no street lights in most of the main areas. They know a great deal about the White South African's way of life, because they work in his houses, factories, offices, clubs and churches and are part of the institutions which he runs. But most White South Africans have never been inside an African's house. But how many middle-class English people have been inside a coal-miner's house?

In the absence of knowledge, myths develop. Newcomers are well advised to take a grain of salt with the tales of African behaviour and customs which they will hear from White South Africans. If they are interested in the subject, the best people to talk to about it are the Africans themselves.

Social contact with them is frowned on by many Whites, but not forbidden officially. However, because of the various group areas and influx laws as well as strange liquor laws, 'immorality' laws and others, newcomers who mix socially with Africans will find it hard to contact them without breaking some law, though it can of course be done.

The Afrikaner's own attitudes to the Blacks is also changing. They used to be called 'kaffers', an insulting term from the Arabic for 'unbeliever', but this is now forbidden. They used to be prohibited from buying liquor, but this has been abolished and the authorities found to their relief, that no great upsurge of drunkenness resulted.

The overall conception of Separate Development, however, is a very interesting experiment – or confidence trick, depending on your point of view – and South Africans are usually prepared to put hundreds of man-hours into discussing it.

3 The Cape

The Cape. 'The fairest Cape in all the world,' said Sir Francis Drake, with British understatement. Along a broken ridge of mountains, up to 4000 feet high, 60 miles long, sea on both sides, lies the Cape Peninsula. The smell of pine-trees and aromatic herbs, the salty wind whipping off the sea. Green and purple bunches of grapes hanging among the vines on blinding white sand. Pine and oak forests, streams, open moorland, great cliffs, a sea that you can see right through to a depth of 30 or 40 feet, from the winding road above. If you walk across the Cape Flats the heathery scrub underfoot gives off a perfume so pungent as to be almost acrid. In the wine cellars the aroma will make you drunk in half an hour if you walk about inhaling deeply. But why rely on inhaling? The wines themselves are marvellous. This is the wine country, the joyous part of South Africa. If you are a teetotaller, now is the time and here is the place to change your life-style.

For climatic reasons, there cannot be a bad year for South African wine; the danger that an early, wet winter will ruin the grapes does not exist – the summer is so long that they are ripe long before the winter is in sight.

If you are a wine enthusiast you must get to the Cape to attend the annual wine show, where some 1500 wines are placed on exhibition, and for a modest fee you can work your way round the exhibits, tasting as many of them as interest you, If you fail to make use of the sawdust-filled barrels between the tables of wines, you had better not be driving.

The wines will range from the very cheap, cloudy, sourish and potent plonk called 'vaaljapie' through decent but modest little wines at very cheap prices, upwards through good wines both white and red at very reasonable prices, from estates usually, but due to be marketed in blended form, and on upwards to excellent wines too good to be blended or exported but entirely consumed in South Africa, and on upwards beyond that to wines so magnificent that no money can buy them, and the only way to get a reliable supply of them is to marry into the family which makes them.

By international standards the prices of wine are very low – comparable to Spain rather than France. The standard of South African *vin ordinaire,* selling in ordinary screw-topped bottles, must be among the highest in the world. It is about double the price of its French equivalent but usually far better quality.

South Africans are great meat eaters, and in the Cape they are fairly good fish and lobster eaters too, though in general they are still waiting to be taught the joys of shellfish and are liable to use for bait what would be delicacies in Spain, Italy or France.

Of course wine-growing is hardly the most important economic activity around the Cape Peninsula – in fact most of it takes place further inland, from about 30 miles away at Paarl, Fransch Hoek where the French settled, and Stellenbosch, on over the mountains towards Wellington, Worcester and the Hex River valley. It is just that it was one of the first and most important industries established in South Africa, and being an occupation which spreads warmth and goodwill, it has helped to mould the whole feeling of the Cape accordingly

The summer climate of the Cape is outrageously warm and balmy; it is perfect for holidays but takes an iron will to spend the whole day at work with the sun blazing down, the white breakers crashing on the beaches, the wind rippling the trees on Table Mountain, the banks of flowers out on the slopes . . .

And indeed, for those able to arrange matters, there is a good deal of quiet sloping off from the office for exceptionally long lunch-hours, stretching in some cases from 11 a.m. until 4 p.m.; Wednesday afternoons taken off for important meetings at the golf-club; Fridays when one has to leave the office just before lunch and can't get back until late on Monday, or possibly Tuesday.

This goes on for at least six months of the year, from November to April, reaching a crescendo of lazy jollity in the really hot months of December and January, when it is really very uncomfortable to do any work at all anyway, unless one happens to be a swimming instructor.

The result, in business circles, is a cheerful, relaxed, rather slow-moving attitude which sometimes sends the tough, hard-driving businessmen from Johannesburg 'up the wall' with frustration trying to get action from their opposite numbers in Cape Town. Frequently they simply take the morning plane at 8 a.m. from Johannesburg, which gets them to Cape Town by about 9.30 a.m, (1000 miles by road, but only 730 in a straight line), do the job themselves and fly back the same evening, exhausted but grimly content.

South Africans love cars; the country has wide-open spaces big enough to make your eyes ache, distances forever and a tradition of movement, exploration and travel that makes people want to get in their cars and zoom off whenever the opportunity can be found. Cape Town is probably the best place in the country for this – the road system is quite frankly magnificent, and it is possible to live in semi-rural surroundings on the side of Tokai mountain, 15 miles from Cape Town, and get to and from one's office in the city in about 25 minutes each way.

Driving in South Africa is more hazardous than in most places in the western world, and newcomers are advised to 'drive defensively' giving way to aggressive South Africans who will insist on overtaking in hideously dangerous places at ridiculous speeds.

They are not quite as savage in Cape Town; Johannesburg driving is terrifying and Pretoria a nightmare – every second car seems to have its backside stove in because people drive a few feet from the car in front, hooting and swerving to and fro and trying to pass when it is not safe.

The best way to arrive in Cape Town is by ship, but it's very fine by air too and if you come by road or rail you will be seeing the mountainous approaches from close up, which is also hard to beat. The view from the sea is of Table Mountain, and in summer there is often the famous 'table-cloth' of rolling cloud coming over the top of the great flat mountain, and pouring down towards the city and then evaporating as it contacts the warmer air lower down. On Devil's Peak at the same time, great swirling clouds will reveal that the retired pirate, Van Hunks, is still keeping up his pipe-smoking competition with the devil. We know – it is a matter of history – that Van Hunks smokes tobacco soaked in rum, but what the devil smokes still awaits scientific investigation.

If you are interested in seafood you need go no further than Cape Town Harbour, where there is a particularly good seafood restaurant serving, among other things, giant deep-sea crabs about a foot in diameter. They dress the diner up in a full-frontal plastic cape before attacking these giant delicacies, to save being splattered with crab-meat if you open them too vigorously. While you are eating, small boats come up to the jetty outside, and tugs will urge you on with hoots of glee. Another good place for Cape rock lobster tails is the open-air restaurant in Cape Town's beautiful gardens, simply but tastefully served at a very reasonable price in surroundings which would be hard to better anywhere in the world.

There are plenty of good restaurants all over South Africa, but while you are in the Cape you should try some traditional Cape dishes, which in fact are much harder to come by than English or French cooking.

Pickled fish is a Cape dish not to be missed: the fish is curried in a deep hot piquant sauce with onion rings. If it is genuine it is very hot and if you are not used to it you will perspire copiously and perhaps even scream a bit, but it is well worth it. Habit-forming. You can often get it at the Railway buffet, but many good Cape hotels and restaurants have it on their menus.

Smoked snoek is delicious: Cape Town's tangy answer to smoked salmon, and very much cheaper. The name snoek for this superb game fish amuses and faintly horrifies the English ear. One can get it in some delicatessens, but my favourite place for it is a little stall called 'Snoekies', at the end of the jetty next to the lobster-canning factory in Hout Bay, eight miles from Cape Town and one of the best drives you will ever experience.

Try to cultivate some Cape Coloured or Cape Malay friends to get invited round to dinner, that's the best way of experiencing a typical Cape curry or a 'snoek smoor', which is snoek braised with potatoes and onions. Tomato bredie is a Cape Afrikaans dish, mutton stewed in fresh tomatoes. Melktert (milk tart) is also an Afrikaans dish which you can buy in any really good bakery – avoid those which do not have it, they know nothing – and is the finest and most delicate specimen of the baking art which the country can offer, it is not to be missed, whether you normally like tarts, milk or not.

Afrikaans cooking started in the Cape, since that's where the Afrikaners themselves began, so it is well established and overlaps with Cape Coloured cooking, which takes in some Malay as well as Dutch, German and English influences. The less said about the influence of English cooking on South African food the better. Some Afrikaners complain about the English burning their farms and putting their women and children in concentration camps during the Boer War, but the introduction of English cooking was, in my view, a far worse outrage and is to be classed with the great disasters which the country has had to withstand, like the phylloxera outbreak among the vines in the last century and rinderpest among the cattle.

Afrikaners have a very good trick with green beans; they chop them and boil them with a peeled potato and an onion in the pot and a lump of butter or mutton fat. They roast mutton with soaked dried apricots and peaches inserted into cuts in the joint. They scoop out a pumpkin and put in a pound of butter, a pound of brown sugar and some cinnamon, put the top back on and roast it slowly in the oven until it begins to cave in through tenderness. They cut leg of mutton into convenient knobs about half the size of a hen's egg, marinate them for a few days in a sauce of curry and dried fruit, then spike them on skewers alternating with onions, green peppers, dried prunes, apple rings and tomatoes and grill them over the red-hot coals of the campfire. It is called sosaties. Don't mess about in a gingerly fashion, have a whole one to yourself if it is offered to you, and don't bother with knives and forks either.

The Afrikaners also invented boerewors (just remember to pronounce the *w* as a *v*, and you'll have spoken your first world in Afrikaans). This is a well-spiced sausage made traditionally from roughly-minced or chopped beef, mutton (you generally get mutton in South Africa, not lamb) and pork in a casing of sheep-gut, in splendid lengths of six feet or more at a time. Do not, in the company of any self-respecting South African eater of any racial or cultural group, suggest that in certain countries boerewors would be padded out with additives of bread or other substances or you will be instantly deported, and quite rightly so. It is cooked by placing a length on the hot wood coals of the campfire and then turning it over after a little while. It can also be put in a pot on the fire, and when it is sizzling well, tossed in some chopped onions, followed shortly by chopped tomatoes (two frequently used staples of good South African cooking) and a glass or so of red wine.

A clove or so of crushed garlic improves the flavour still further. At the same time get an Afrikaner, or an African – both are equally expert – to show you how to cook a pot of 'stywe pap' (maizemeal, known as mealie-meal, cooked very firm and almost dry). You break off pieces of the mealie-meal and dip it into the sauce and eat it with the sausage. If you are thinking of settling in the Cape, it might be as well to get a Cape drinker at the same time, to show you the trick of lifting a gallon-jar of red wine on the crook of your arm with a forefinger through its lug, so that there is no need to bother with glasses or mugs.

This kind of cooking will of course be done at the outdoor barbecue, or *braaivleis,* which South Africans love and to which they will be delighted to introduce you. If you are a keen meat-eater, you will be delighted too. If you are a vegetarian, you had better hide in a darkened room with a handful of nuts.

On the first of January Cape Town becomes possessed by the Coon Carnival, a sort of mass open-air Black and White Minstrel Show, in which tens of thousands of Coloured people take to the streets in fancy dress and dance and sing their way from one side of the peninsula to the other. It is one of the world's great folk festivals, rivalled for size, spontaneity and exuberance only by the Mardi Gras in Rio de Janeiro.

There are also a variety of more sophisticated entertainments, some reasonable theatre, some rather good ballet, opera and music. Films are heavily censored throughout the country, as are publications. However, times are changing and attributes relaxing.

There are flower-sellers in Adderly Street, and open-air stalls at a flea-market on the Grand Parade opposite the City Hall on Saturday mornings – well-stocked and well-attended. Long Street is one of the most interesting and varied streets in Cape Town, with fine old Cape buildings with wrought-iron balconies on either side, a variety of interesting shops and a particularly well-run traditional Turkish bath, for which the municipality are much to be congratulated.

For active sightseers, a good morning's walk round central Cape Town would be to start at the Castle, the country's first important building built betwen 1666 and 1679. It is worth a visit; the dungeons are most impressive and to cheer you up after seeing them there is a fine collection of antiques and paintings: indigenous antiquities from the coming of white people onwards are called Afrikana.

Then from there, stroll along to Adderley Street: if it is a Saturday you will pass through the open-air market, and the collection of fruit-stalls on the western side is worth a stop. Wander among the flower-selling Coloured women in Adderley Street – they are actually in a small side-street called Trafalgar Place, just off the centre of Adderley Street but easy to find. You might note that not all Coloured people are picturesque and charming, some of them are ruffians – known as skollies – so watch your wallet, lock your car and don't leave tempting cameras in it, especially in central Cape Town.

Turn left in Adderley Street and after a few blocks you will pass the country's oldest church – the Dutch Reformed Goote Kerk (1704), it has a very fine carved pulpit by Anton Anreith. Then when the road swings round sharply to the right, you continue up the pedestrians-only Government Avenue shaded with oak-trees, and passing Parliament on your left and 15 acres of superb gardens on your right. Just a few hundred yards from Adderley Street the traffic noise fades away and is replaced by the cooing of doves – a very typical Cape sound, and grey squirrels dart up and will take peanuts from your hand. You can get tea or lunch in the Gardens and then go on further up Government Avenue – it is one kilometre long – and you will find a hothouse with a tremendous collection of flowers, an art gallery on your left (it's good too), with the avenue broadening out to a wide terrace with ornamental pond and statues in it.

If you want to keep your walk down to a more modest length, then turn right at this point – west, facing Lion's Head – and make your way out of Government Avenue and the gardens, through a couple of intervening small streets into Long Street, which runs parallel to Government Avenue. Walk up the left side to where it forks at the top, and then back down the right-hand side, and you will have seen, in two or three hours leisurely stroll with several stops, some of the best that Cape Town has to offer.

If you like fine eighteenth-century houses and are interested in the indigenous craftsmanship there are a couple of superb houses open to the public, more or less on your route – the Old Town House in Longmarket Street on Greenmarket Square, and the Martin Melck and Koopmans de Wet Houses in Strand Street.

A few streets further up towards Lion's Head and Signal Hill is the remnants of the Malay quarter, which also has some interesting and gracious houses of a typical Cape style, though privately owned.

Now if you want to go further afield and you are a newcomer, you have a clear choice. There is good public transport, plenty of brochures, several car-hire firms and organised coach excursions. You can make use of those facilities and you are not likely to be disappointed. But if you have any South African contacts – and they are not difficult to acquire, the natives are friendly – then you can in general rely on considerable hospitality. You should ask your relatives, friends or business contacts if they can spare a few hours to show you around, and tell them the kind of thing you are specially interested in, whether it be landscapes, seascapes, Cape architecture, sports or whatever, and they will have their own ideas and ways of introducing you to their country, better, because more personal, than any guidebook could be. If you want to reciprocate and cannot offer hospitality in return, then small gifts are always appreciated.

Unless they are very exotic, personal or special there is not much point in bringing gifts with you from other countries, because South African shops are very well stocked with both local and imported goods.

There is a long list of interesting and attractive things to look at in and around Cape Town: beautiful landscaping along the motorway leading past Groote Schuur Hospital (of heart-transplant fame); the other Groote Schuur where the Prime Minister lives when Parliament is in session; the perfectly situated and impressive University; a small but fine zoo, and then – a must, this, Kirstenbosch Botanical Gardens on the eastern slopes of Table Mountain, which enjoys, like most things around Cape Town, a magnificent mountain setting, and happens to be one of the world's really important botanic collections.

If you have more time, you can go on to Groot Constantia, built by Simon van der Stel, where they still make fine wines. Just near Kirstenbosch, to the left of the road on top of a hill, you will be passing the remains of a wild almond thicket planted by Jan van Riebeek in about 1668, intended to keep the Hottentots out of South Africa. If you go on down to Muizenberg you will pass through Tokai, where there are still some fine old wine-farms dating from the 1600's, although there are also some extensive new housing estates which have sprung up between them in recent years.

At Cape Town you look out onto the cold Atlantic Ocean

and the icy Benguela current which sweeps up from the Antarctic, now at Muizenberg you are looking at the Indian Ocean, and the difference in temperature is quite startling.

At Clifton Beach, on the other side of the moutnain, your feet and ankles will ache with the pain of the icy water when you venture in for a swim, however hot the day, but at Muizenberg, in False Bay, the water in midsummer can be 80° Fahrenheit – almost stickily warm by contrast. But for sunbathing purposes Clifton Beach is better – it doesn't catch the ferocious south-easter, which can blow at near hurricane force for days on end. False Bay gets it and so does Cape Town itself. If it's going full blast when you're there, the best thing is to reflect that it is called the Cape Doctor, and is blowing all the bugs and pollution out of the air, out to sea and away from you.

Going on down the peninsula, a couple of miles beyond Muizenberg you reach Kalk Bay, which is a delightful little fishing harbour, well worth a closer look and if you're lucky enough to time your visit to catch the small boats unloading, there is always a special excitement in seeing what the fishermens' nets have brought in. You can usually buy fresh fish on the spot too.

Simonstown is another six miles on down the Peninsula, and of course a famous name which crops up whenever the strategic role of South Africa in the western military system is discussed. You may wonder how this sleepy little port, rather like a village in Cornwall, could be of any critical significance in controlling the Indian Ocean in a global conflict in which the navies, missiles, air forces and nuclear submarines of the great powers were embroiled.

It is probably better to shrug off such speculations and press on towards the Cape of Good Hope Nature Reserve. There is quite a good variety of wildlife in this little reserve which is not so very little either, being 30 miles square. It takes up the whole point of the Peninsula, which looks and feels like the southernmost point of the whole continent of Africa, though in fact it isn't (Cape Agulhas is). It is very well worth toiling up the steep hill to Cape Point peak to stare dizzily down at the gigantic waves crashing on the rocks hundreds of feet below. As a boy, I once spent a night in that lighthouse, reading Dracula.

Then you must return to Cape Town up the other side of the Peninsula, where the best place for a longer stop is Hout Bay, a mixture of a fishing village and a colony of fairly rich, artistic people. On the winding avenue leading up to Constantia Nek there is a little shop in a small ancient building on the left where they sell farm produce, home-made grape jam and a very good fudge.

If you are interested in wine then there are a number of beautiful towns where it is made, surrounded by the vineyards. One of them is Fransch Hoek, where French immigrants settled because they were Huguenot Protestants, persecuted at one stage in their own country but welcomed in Calvinist South Africa from about 1688 onwards. They were actively discouraged from keeping up their language, which seems a pity, but they applied their agricultural and wine-making knowlege and settled in very well. Many leading Afrikaans families with names like du Toit, De Villiers and so on are descended from them. The hinterland near Cape Town, the Western Province, is famous for fruit-growing, and is also the country's granary. The combination of wheat-fields, mountains, vineyards, fruit orchards and the sea in the distance provides a landscape of such gripping beauty that you may find you will stay there and never want to leave, but even if you do manage to tear yourself away, it will haunt you and call you back for the rest of your life.

The main wine town is Paarl, about 35 miles from Cape Town on the main northern motorway. This is where the great wine co-operative, the KWV, has its headquarters and cellars, and it is worth a visit. There is an interesting long day's circular drive if you go via Fransch Hoek – not a very beautiful town, but lying in a fine valley with an interesting monument to the Huguenots – and then climb the Fransch Hoek pass on the Villersdorp road just beyond the town.

This is one of the country's oldest passes to the interior and is still known as the 'Olifantspad' (elephant road), because it was a track much used by wildlife when the first white settlers arrived on the scene, and they later turned it into a wagon trail and eventually a road.

From the top of the pass there is a fine view of the Drakenstein valley in which Fransch Hoek lies, and then on the other side the scenery becomes much more wild and rugged as the road twists down. These mountains often have snow on them for several months during the winter. At the bottom of the pass there is a bridge and a junction where you should turn right, taking the road not to Villersdorp, but to Grabouw, also known as Elgin. Then there is another very fine and interesting mountainous drive through apple-farming country into Elgin or Grabouw (the town is called Grabouw but the district is known in many apple-importing countries as Elgin.)

From there you go back to Cape Town via yet another very big and spectacular pass – Sir Lowry's Pass – looking down over the whole of False Bay and the Cape Flats, with the entire line of the Peninsula's mountains stretching across from left to right, 25 miles away.

If you have any energy left you will find it worthwhile going back to Cape Town via Somerset West and the University town of Stellenbosch.

It was agreed when the country was formed in 1910 by uniting the Cape, Free State, Natal and Transvaal, that the Government would be in Pretoria but Parliament would be in Cape Town, so each year the Government entrains with all its files, secretaries, wives and children, and comes to Cape Town for six months for the Parliamentry session. During this time nothing much can be done or decided in the line of Government business in Pretoria, because all the heads of departments are in Cape Town, and the reverse is true for Cape Town when the Government goes back to Pretoria. But Cape Town lives an autonomous life of its own, tending to regard the influx of civil servants and politicians as one of nature's little trials, like the South-Easter, whereas Pretoria is very much a Government city and feels their presence or absence much more keenly.

There is a well-developed industrial and financial community in Cape Town, although the Stock Exchange is in Johannesburg. Cape Town is the legislative capital, Pretoria the administrative capital, Johannesburg the financial capital and Bloemfontein, in the Orange Free State, the judicial capital. They are of course also regional centres for provinces the size of West European countries, so that they all have well-developed communication and distributive systems, primary and secondary industry to varying extents, and all the other services which one would expect in properly developed cities.

6 Columns of the Rhodes Memorial, Cape Town

4 The West Coast

And now for something completely different. Because of the way the winds and currents work, it is the Eastern side of South Africa that gets the rain, while the West is spectacularly dry – and the two different aspects converge at Cape Town. So if you go east you will see the fruit orchards, wheat fields, vineyards and lush groves of wellgrown trees, but if you go up the west coast, within five or ten miles of the city you will find yourself in a very different climatic region, arid, sandy, tough, much less populated but with a deep fascination of its own.

It is by no means desert – you have to go further up the coast for that – but the trees are smaller, the vegetation spikier, the farms fewer and tending to grow wheat rather than fruit trees or vines, so that the aspect is more typically that of long rolling hills of glittering wheat in between white sand and dense, very dark green indigenous scrub bushland. By no means unattractive, but the light is fiercely clear; if you are not wearing dark glasses your face muscles will begin to ache from screwing up your eyes against the glare, and your photographs are very likely to be over-exposed.

By the time you have got to Blaauwbergstrand, some 12 miles from Cape Town, you will already be getting into the hard, arid side of South Africa and if you want to get the feel of the whole country this is probably essential: much more than half of it is semi-desert, vast tracts of silent, open land baking in the relentless blaze of the sun. Some people have a certain taste for deserts, and they will find much pleasure here. Most South Africans think of 'the countryside' as great, open spaces stretching on for hundreds of miles with scarcely a soul in

7 *'Cape Town Dutch'. The house known as 'Groot Constantia'*

them and tend to feel very claustrophobic when they go abroad and find themselves in densely-populated areas of Europe or elsewhere. They are even incredulous when English guides insist that the busy landscape they are seeing, for example in South East England, is in fact regarded in England as countryside.

You must press on far beyond Blaauwberg, though, to get to grips with the Western dry side of the country – and it has much more to offer than drought and heat. For example before you get to the really dry country you will come to Mamre, which is a mainly Coloured hamlet getting on for two centuries old, established originally by Moravian missionaries. It is a quiet country village with plenty of trees, gardens and quiet shady streets. Make allowances when driving through, for sudden encounters with old men driving donkeys, and chickens crossing the road. Some Coloured families base themselves here although commuting to work in Cape Town. They might leave the children here for grannie to look after while they are working in the city, and eventually retire here themselves.

My favourite place on this entire coast is Saldanha Bay, which is about 95 miles from Cape Town. The attraction is the great bay itself, with the 10-mile-long lagoon to its south known as Langebaan. If you prefer the company of a minimum of people then the place to head for is not Langebaan Village and Saldanha Bay town, but the western peninsula which sticks out between the lagoon and the sea – the road to it will be marked Donkergat (Dark Hole, literally, though it's anything but). Donkergat is an abandoned whaling station, and the peninsula is now a nature reserve. The lagoon is perfect for yachting, and great numbers of sea-birds and waterfowl breed there and on the small islands in the bay, which are a famous source of guano – dried bird's manure, a valuable fertilizer. (At one stage, in 1844, more than 300 ships were in the Bay to gather guano for export).

On the Donkergat side of the lagoon you will pass some really old Cape houses, fishermen's cottages dating from the 1700's, dotted along by the waterside and looking very peaceful indeed, though the bay itself had a remarkably turbulent history in the early days of settlement. French, Dutch and English all contended for it at various stages, and there were even some modest naval battles fought in its sheltered waters, which must have astounded the Hottentot inhabitants on the shore.

On the Western promontory, or peninsula, it is wild and isolated and you can get right down into rocky coves and onto sandy beaches where few people have been until very recently.

Across the water, Saldanha Bay itself is a well-established little old fishing town, but on the threshold of great growth as it becomes the centre for a new iron-ore port, shipping ore from Sishen, far inland. It still presents a great stretch of tranquil bay and clean white beach many miles long, with clear water lapping in small waves, but this is no doubt going to give way to a much more man-influenced environment as the iron-shipping facilities develop.

The coastline gets progressively more arid and the road leads through country of a burnt-out grandeur as you go northwards up the western side of South Africa. There are some towns of charm in fertile valleys, like Citrusdal and Clanwilliam on the way, but the farming gives way from wheat to scattered sheep among sparse bush and granite outcrops and by the time you have reached Springbok it is no longer farm products, but the minerals of the earth itself which are the attraction for man to be there at all.

On the way you will have climbed a spectacular pass about 20 miles north of Vanrhynsdorp – Van Rhyn's Pass – which climbs and climbs for miles, to a height of 2,700 feet above sea level, rewarding you with a magnificent view of the great Namaqualand plains below. The time to be there is spring – about October, but it varies – when if there has been rain the entire vast landscape will be covered with Namaqualand daisies, and you will have seen one of the truly great sights of Africa, and you will never forget it.

You will go through terrible forgotten little towns like Garies (a Hottentot name, like many others in this region) and Nuwerus, lying among menacing granite crags and sweltering in the sun. If you want a foretaste of hell, try this route in December, when the temperatures reach 120° Fahrenheit.

But there is an excitement about the landscape, too. Many of the stones you look at when you stop are not stones at all, but minute succulent plants adapted to live in an area where the rainfall is an inch or so in a good year. The children here will have seen very few animals and hardly any plants, but they will talk about mica, copper and tourmaline, and tell you they have found a private supply of tiger's eye. There is an immense quantity of 'rare earth' and of semi-precious stones, almost as if they were leading one on to the diamonds themselves which lie 100 miles beyond Springbok, in great, jealously-guarded tracts along the most impossibly barren landscape of all – the Skeleton Coast.

Walking in the hills near Springbok one day I came upon a large lump of almost pure mica about four feet square and three feet high, and was quite excited by it, thinking it must be valuable. But a local 12 year-old child who was with me said: 'No, no – we call that burnt mica, it's got no commercial value – very poor quality.'

Sometimes the people in those parts are nearly as wild as the landscape. As I was changing a tyre outside the hotel in the little main square of Springbok I met Isak. He must have been drinking a lot, because he fell down next to me, completely flat on his face and then from that position he said: 'Good evening, can I help you?'

I thanked him politely and said I could manage and we struck up a conservation, with Isak continuing to lie flat on his face, though talking quite fluently. 'What do you do for a living?' 'I smuggle diamonds,' he said, 'and I've just come out of jail.' I gave him a lift home, to a shack which he shared with a woman whose husband was away on the diggings, three or four children, two old people and several goats. They confirmed that he was a diamond smuggler, but the old lady said he wasn't very good at it, and almost always got caught.

He would vanish for weeks on end into the barren mountainous country and the endless, baking plains with their scattered piles of rock. He generally wore a pair of old dancing pumps and the remains of a suit, and did not seem to carry any provisions or equipment for these journeys in search of diamonds and diamond-deals. Sometimes he came back very hungry and thirsty and the old woman said that on one such occasion when he got back he finished off five tins of fish and a bottle of methylated spirits, all by himself.

In Springbok I also met a very gentle and well-read old gentleman, in his seventies, who told me that he only spent half of the year in Springbok, buying semi-precious stones and a specialised range of minerals. The other half of the year he apparently spent in his offices just off Piccadilly in London, selling them.

Beyond Springbok the road leads on to cross the Orange River into South West Africa, or Namibia – which is another story. But if you want a glimpse of the terrible coast of skeletons and diamonds, the nearest point would be Port Nolloth. It is not recommended for the faint-hearted, but if you have a taste for deserts, for starkness, for the bizarre in landscapes, then it is worth the sweat – and whichever way you travel there, you will sweat.

You will go down a mountain pass, the Anenous, about 35 miles out of Springbok, where gigantic boulders lie scattered. Another striking feature of the road from the Anenous Pass down to the coastal plain is the large number of big, fat puff-adders which you will find lying in the road. If you count the puff-adders in, say, five miles of road, and then work out the length of the road multiplied by its width, you will be able to calculate, and then contemplate, how many puff-adders per acre there are in that area, and unless you are specially fond of puff-adders, you will probably not wish to stop and picnic thereabouts, but it is interesting to have passed through.

About 10 miles before Port Nolloth the road begins to offer you a switchback ride over a series of wavelike dunes, and if you choose the right speed this is quite thrilling, but if you go too fast you will fly off the top of one dune and land in the trough of the next, which is to be avoided.

You will know when you are just about to get into Port

Nolloth because there will almost certainly be thick waves of clammy mist hanging over it, scented with rotting fish. The entrance to the town passes a disused cemetery and an abandoned narrow-gauge railway-line.

If, having crossed 100 miles or so of arid country, you have built up a thirst, you are advised to call for cold beer. The local water has a penetrating, sickly-sweet taste which even permeates the local bread and eggs. You need not worry about the flavour of the local vegetables – they do not exist.

There is a fishing factory and a small harbour, and the fishermen who use it have to know their business, because the icy Benguela current in which they catch their crayfish and pilchards comes straight up from the Antarctic, and it can be a killer. You will have several hundred miles of rather fine beach very much to yourself. If you try swimming in the water and unless you are already in the habit of swimming regularly in the northern part of the Hudson Bay or the Bering Straits, you will be incredulous at how cold it is.

Spend a day and a night there, and get talking to people who have lived there all their lives. The talk will tend to be about fishing and about diamonds, and often very fascinating. If you try to go on from here towards the diamond fields you will need a special permit, which generally speaking you cannot get. The diamonds are not for taking.

When they were first found Port Nolloth was the centre of a diamond rush, but the fields were rapidly taken over by small consortia, and the Government declared the rest 'State Diggings' and put a stop to individual prospecting in the area. So great was the rage of the 'little men' who had gathered to try for their fortune when they found that most of it was already in the hands of a few 'big men', that in 1928 thousands of them threatened to storm the diggings and police set up machine-guns to keep them out; their rage petered out in arguments among themselves and the area remains prohibited.

If, just after Springbok, you turn right instead of left and head east, you will be heading for Upington. The road is hard going but the scenery is spectacular in a deserted and arid way. There are no animals, no people, and no signs of life in sight as far as the horizon for hour after hour of steady driving. You might like to stop and have a good scream somewhere along this road. Nobody will mind.

There are some attractive small settlements on the Orange River, growing excellent fruit by pumping water from the great stream, as at Keimoes and Kakamas. Kakamas was originally a settlement for 'poor whites', but is much more prosperous now.

'Poor whites' play an important part in the culture and running of South Africa. Many of them were people who came from farming families that went gradually broke, usually from a combination of bad luck and bad farming, but some of them because of the British 'scorched earth' tactics in the Boer War. They drifted into the towns and cities, without skills, to get themselves jobs in the civil service or industry, and official policy was that they had to be looked after so that they would not sink down to the level of the black people of the country. Government jobs, such as white labourers' jobs on the South African Railways, were created for them and subsidized 'sub-economic housing,' and certain philanthropic architects and building contractors made fine fortunes out of such schemes, in the South African style. Job reservation laws and practices preserve the lion's share of semi-skilled jobs for them, against the competition of the blacks.

Around the Upington area, known as Gordonia, you will encounter the biggest Afrikaners in the country – and therefore some of the biggest people in the world. They have been renowned for their great size for some centuries now, but some combination of selective breeding and climate seems to have concentrated the hugest specimens around the Gordonia district. Fortunately they are generally friendly and peaceful these days.

5 The East Coast and the Garden Route

Those of us – I number myself among them – who love deserts are a minority, but no normal human being could fail to find the Eastern Cape movingly beautiful. It is this side of South Africa which gets the rain, and the difference it makes to the landscape compared with the dry west could not be more striking. Great deep forests, lagoons with dense undergrowth growing right down to the water's edge, luscious meadows – the land of the long summer, where the living is much, much easier.

It is a very full landscape, eventful, rapidly changing, crowded with interest. Let us look at a few of my favourite places on a trip through it, and then you should go into it yourself and you will find your own – it has something for everybody. People who live in this part of South Africa seem to enjoy themselves more, and make full use of their leisure – especially if they like fishing, walking, sunbathing, swimming, mountain-climbing, gardening, riding, driving or anything that is better done outdoors.

On the way east from Cape Town lies Caledon, which is a spa whose waters are highly rated among connoisseurs of natural hot baths. It lies in wheat-growing country where wheat-farmers work like men possessed for months on end, putting in 16 hour days to get their wheat in and then going off, well-laden with provisions and fishing tackle, to take long, well-earned holidays by the sea at places like Gansbaai, Hermanus and that whole superb, varied coastline.

My friend Japie grows many hillsides full of wheat near there, as his father and grandfather did before him. When my wife suggested after breakfast that she might take a walk round the farm, he looked at her thoughtfully and said after a while, 'yes, well that will take you about three days.'

Caledon has a superb wild-flower garden. If you are interested in wild flowers you had better allow at least half a day for wandering in this landscaped but informal 25-acre display. South Africans, like Texans, believe that a great many things in their country are among the biggest and best in the world, and in this case they are right.

Fishing villages along this coast, like Gansbaai, are holiday resorts as well as places where people have been living for centuries, farming, fishing and trading, so they are well-established little towns and they stay alive when the visitors disappear in the winter. Hermanus has a charming little scolloped-out fishing harbour cut in the cliffside just below the town, which is also a very fine swimming place. It takes its character as a town from the number of older, wealthier people who have retired there, but it can liven up considerably when the young bloods come in to whoop it up on a Saturday night, especially during the summer.

You are still just facing east, in the Western Province at this stage, but you are well into the lush climatic area. Going on along this route (a splendid highway, the N2), it's well worth turning off the main road at Riversdale and driving down the 25 odd miles to Puntjie, in St Sebastian Bay, to see the strange thatched dwellings known as kapsteilhuisies which farming families have built for themselves as holiday cottages there. They look like reconstructions of the type of thatched huts found near marshes in Europe more than 1000 years ago, and the first farmers to put them up there did so quite spontaneously, combining the local building materials – or lack of them – with a long-persisting tribal memory of such dwellings rigged up by their ancestors in Europe. They have been preserved and the owners of the land, displaying a typically Cape love of tradition, have insisted for some time that only these kapsteilhuisies may be built on this piece of the coast.

It is a bit off the main tourist route, so the facilities will be slim or non-existent. If you like getting away from crowds, get a large-scale map of the area, take your own camping gear and look for stretches of the coast not reached by the roads – a walk of half a mile or so off the beaten track will repay you. (But if you find yourself going through somebody's farm gate, go to the farmhouse and ask for permission to continue, as well as directions – you will seldom be refused either.)

Mossel Bay is another town well worth a stop-over, whether you are camping or staying in hotels. This was the first land sighted by Bartolemu Dias when he rounded the Cape, and what a pleasant surprise it must have been after the daunting desert coast which he had encountered on the way down the western side of Africa. The natives were not particularly friendly, however, and threw stones at him and his men. They may have had a premonition of the kind of deal their descendants were going to get from the newcomers. In recent times, for example, they have been forbidden to sell fish to visitors, who may only buy it from one or two fortunate Whites who have the required licences.

In recent years the urge to make money quickly seems to have spread in South Africa – partly a function of increasing numbers and partly the belief among many Whites that 'it can't last much longer – make your fortune while the going is good.' In general, this get-rich-quick spirit, with all that it entails in the way of hasty service, shoddy goods, overcrowding, irritability, noise and a generally 'plastic' life-style, is to be encountered more at the newer, brighter, brasher holiday resorts which have grown up too fast, too soon, like the ones strung out along the coast south of Durban. Many people obviously enjoy them and find their facilities convenient and familiar – it is a matter of taste – but it is as well to know where to find them or how to avoid them, depending on what you are looking for.

Mossel Bay, anyway, is relatively free of that sort of atmosphere, although it is a popular resort and smacks of commercialism.

Further on around the sweep of the great bay lies George, sleepy, oak-shaded, a kind and restful town and a favourite retiring place. It was founded in 1811 and named after George III, the Cape being a Colony at the time. The first landdrost (local magistrate) with wisdom and great foresight, decreed that the main streets were to be 300 feet wide, with trees on both sides, creating a spacious character which has persisted and flourished.

It has been a timber-producing town for 150 years and for the last 80 years or so there has fortunately been a re-afforestation programme for the area, to prevent the indigenous trees being wiped out. I met one wealthy young man from George who said his family farmed there. Later on he revealed what they farmed – stinkwood trees. They take 150 years to mature, so the pace of the family's farming is not too exhausting.

From Mossel Bay onwards to Knysna the road passes, or crosses over, some spectacular coastal lakes and lagoons, and their shallow warm waters are a whole world in themselves, with their own abundant plant-life, fishes and crustaceans, waterfowl, and indeed the people who live around them and off them too.

Inland from George and Knysna lie the Cango Caves – another instance of 'biggest and best' – and well worth a visit. Revisiting as an adult I found them just as breathtaking as the time I first saw them as a small boy. They have vast chambers, tiny tunnels, great underground gorges leading away into blackness, magical groupings of stalactites (they're the ones which have to hang on tight, so as not to fall off the roof) and stalagmites (they might one day reach the top – that is how my father taught me to remember which is which) like fairy organ-pipes, and others folded into weird and exotic shapes, like magician's pulpits, cauldrons, thrones and jewel-chambers.

It is quite exciting, especially for younger, more agile, people to scramble up the last section through a narrow, steep tunnel, but this treat is optional. (It's not that difficult though, I once went through it with a crippled friend who managed it using just his arms and shoulders.)

Near the Cango Caves is the Swartberg Pass. For real

contrast this should be approached from the Little Karroo side, from the sweet little town of Prince Albert, with its irrigation furrows running alongside the streets to water each person's garden in strict rotation. The Little Karroo is usually blindingly hot, except in winter when it is only very hot (during the day – at night it's another story). But in mid-winter, when the sun may be blazing down on Prince Albert at the foot of the pass, there can be several feet of snow high up in the pass itself, blocking the road in a manner which children will find most entertaining – especially South African children who may never have seen snow before.

Prince Albert is a kind town. If you've been ill, particularly if there has been anything wrong with your chest, go and stay there for a few months. The people are friendly and find strangers interesting, and most of them can speak quite good English, though they may be a little shy about it. There's a well-stocked little library, the school has a tradition of providing a very sound education, and fruit grows very well here too. It is probably very like other little Karroo towns – it's just that one small boy with a weak chest 30 years ago became very fond of Prince Albert. The only complaint against the place is that they might give you stewed guavas for breakfast – an acquired taste which some will never acquire.

Back on the side where George and Knysna lie, we move on to Knysna and pass the ostrich farms around Ondtshoorn. The ostrich is a curious bird – a very fast runner, with its short wings and long legs, and vicious too. About 70 years ago, when my grandmother was teaching small Hottentot children the King's English at a mission school in the Karroo, she once saw an ostrich kick a herd-boy to death. Their legs hinge up forward from the knee and on their middle toe is a claw about three inches long, so if you want to try an ostrich egg it is better to take it when the ostrich is not looking. It's for the bigger eater, being equivalent to about 24 hen's eggs.

Why do they farm them? Well in Victorian and Edwardian times the women wanted the feathers for their hats, and that started it. Then South Africans found that ostrich-meat makes very good, dry, flaky biltong and since the chewing of biltong is the national addiction, they farm ostriches as much for their meat now as their feathers. Biltong is salted, spiced, wind-dried raw meat. It should be so dry that it will snap like a bit of wood, and you need wildebeest, ostrich or springbok for that. Beef biltong is the most common, but the true addict demands game biltong.

Knysna has one of the greatest, most magnificant lagoons, and it comes in through two great crags of rock called Knysna Heads. In the lagoon there is an oyster-hatchery where they cultivate oysters in racks of boxes. You can order them from elsehwere in the country and they will deliver them by rail to anywhere in South Africa, wrapped in wet seaweed which keeps them not only fresh but alive for about eight days. They are graded by sizes, and by international standards the prices are reasonable. They used to be cheap, but those days seem to be past. Cape rock lobsters (crayfish) also used to be so plentiful and cheap that until quite recently their price was about on a level with mince-meat. Then the export trade built up more and more and people with political connections moved into the fishing concessions; breeding grounds were fished out and today you pay about the same for lobster in Cape Town as you do in London. There may be a moral in it somewhere.

Knysna itself is a beautifully situated town, between the forested mountains and the sea, and straggles about amiably with no great evidence of planning.

Although its best-known industry throughout the country is the production of oysters, the people of the town, show little awareness of them and if you try to order them in local bars and restaurants you are likely to meet with blank stares. In general, South Africans are exceedingly conservative about seafood. They like fresh fish and they love lobster, but as for inkfish, the spiky sea urchins known as 'sea eggs', white sand-mussels, crabs – if you like them you will probably have them all to yourself. Even mussels were very rarely eaten until recently – possibly because they are occasionally subject in these waters to a travelling infection which makes them poisonous. I remember asking a maitre d'hotel about that in a

Cape Town hotel where they had them on the menu, and he said, 'oh yes, they can be very poisonous. As a matter of fact we've had five deaths since I've been here, from them – but they're delicious, would you like some?'

The Knysna forests have native Cape elephants in them and families of woodcutters who have lived there in isolation so long that they have inter-married over many generations, with some strange genetic results. They are one of the legends of South African verbal folklore not mentioned in official guide-books – though no doubt many of them are fine, upstanding, genetically normal citizens.

They used to cut down the indigenous trees on a free-for-all basis, until it was realised that they would soon destroy the magnificent forests which are very scarce in South Africa and mostly concentrated in this area. Then the government brought in controls and the woodcutter familes were allowed to draw lots for trees selected by the Forestry Department. Now they are not allowed to cut wood privately any more in the area, forestry being strictly controlled.

The South African forestry department is an admirable institution, combining some quaint old hierarchical traditions inherited from the original ex-Indian army British colonists who founded it, with modern techniques and enlightened attitudes towards both the science of forestry and the people who work with forests and for the department. In recent years they have been handing over some areas of forest to various tribal authorities as part of the separate development programme. They have taken a pride in handing them over in excellent running order, to African staff whom they have trained up to the highest levels. Their work has a spirit of enthusiasm combined with high standards of achievement which is most refreshing, especially for one arriving from some of the more tired parts of Europe.

The forestry department is a major employer of African labour, and in this often very sensitive area they have also achieved some interesting breakthroughs. To take one random example: in one large timber works in a forest area they had an enormous absenteeism problem, as well as a turnover of more than 100 per cent a year in their workforce. None of the text-book methods of dealing with these problems made the slightest impression. So they put the whole problem in the hands of one man and gave him carte blanche to work on it. He was an old ex-policeman, who spoke several African languages. He started methodically working through the hundreds orsistent absentees, calling them in and questioning them carefully and not unsympathetically, when they came back to work.

He found that in some cases they had to take a day off to go and cope with one of the endless pieces of paper-work which beset black people in South Africa – work permits, residence permits, poll taxes or whatever it may be. He realized that if he got a clerk in the works to deal with this paperwork for them when it came up, then that particular problem would be solved. He found that sometimes they had to take a sick child or wife off to see a doctor or be attended to at a clinic – so he arranged for a nurse to be available on the spot to handle that problem, and absenteeism dropped another few notches. Then he found that one of the worst days for absenteeism was Wednesdays for no apparent reason – the weekend hangover was gone, there was no tempting beer drink or social function to attend, they just stayed away.

Head office took this one up and they found eventually that dietary deficiency was behind it – the workers were not getting enough to eat in relation to their strenuous physical work, and by mid-week they were literally so drained and exhausted that many of them simply stayed home to recover. This was solved by giving everybody a pint of nourishing soup every day, in mid-morning, regardless of what they had to eat at home. Absenteeism dropped a substantial number of notches further. Gradually all the key causes keeping men away from work were pinpointed and dealt with and today the plant has an exceptionally stable labour force, well above the average for the area and the type of work. Paternalistic, if you like, but it works.

So the forests you will be passing through on this Garden Route are not running themselves – although some of the trees have been there 2,000 years – they are in fact being looked after by a very active and devoted organisation of foresters.

For many South Africans this is the favourite holiday coast and you will find collections of holiday shacks, chalets, bungalows and occasionally mansions, depending on what the owners can afford, at many points between George and Port Elizabeth. Plettenberg Bay is a particularly famous one, so perhaps you might like to avoid it and look for something less popular. If so, you have hundreds of miles of coastline with dozens of little seaside settlements scattered along it and the best way to find out which one you like best is to go there and give yourself time to wander along that coast, stopping at hotels, motels or camping sites – you have a plentiful choice of them all, right along the Garden Route. Talk to local people, and use the official guide-books too – they are excellently produced.

The few surviving elephants in the Knysna forest are of special interest, because they are the last of a separate race of elephants. But they are hard to find and though you may come across one of their very impressive droppings while walking in the great forests, the chances are against you encountering one of the giants himself.

However, they do have several dozen relatives living much more visibly on the same route, at the Addo National Park, 43 miles from Port Elizabeth, and there are special viewing spots in the park near feeding places where you can get a close-up view of the elephants. They were nearly exterminated by a professional hunter in the early 1920's because of the damage they had done to local farms, but at the last moment, when there were only about 15 out of 150 left, the public conscience awoke and they were saved. After years of hard work by devoted elephant-lovers the present well-run park was achieved. One of the great difficulties was how to keep the elephants in it, and this was ingeniously solved by using second-hand lift cables for the perimeter fence, with second-hand tramlines for the uprights. Try and break through that.

The park has not only elephants, but a complete collection of Cape antelopes, walking about freely in their natural

8 Northern Transvaal landscape at Magoebaskloof

surroundings.

Apart from the world-famous, and somewhat overcrowded, though excellently-run Kruger Park, there are of course dozens of smaller first-class wildlife parks like the Addo scattered throughout the country.

When you get to Port Elizabeth there are two great attractions – the snake park and the dolphinarium. There are many other places of interest too, of course, like the monument to the horses who died in the Boer war, and the tower called the Campanile in memory of the 1820 British settlers, where you can climb the spiral staircase for exercise and the view. But the snake park is a must, and so is the dolphinarium, and fortunately they are next door to each other.

The dolphins are trained to leap through hoops, ring bells with their snouts, and perform various other feats, a spectacular demonstration which they seem to enjoy as much as the crowds. They have bigger brains than people and since they are given a fish for performing each item on their repertoire, it may well be that they take the view that it is they who have trained the human attendants and have the better half of the deal.

The snake park has one of the largest and most comprehensive collections of snakes in Africa, and they are exhibited and explained by a magnificent looking Xhosa in whipcord breeches and jackboots, who knows his subject well and appears to enjoy their company. He is wary about handling extremely venomous puff-adders and does not handle the horribly venomous mambas at all; the mambas are behind plate-glass, and the notice on their case says, among other things, that those who are bitten by them usually have a maximum of ten minutes to live. South Africans who have lived in mamba areas (sub-tropical generally) will delight in telling you stories of people and animals who have not survived even that long after an encounter with a mamba. They are said to be able to catch a man on a galloping horse, but this is almost certainly untrue, in the sense that they would not bother if they missed him on the first strike, which

9 Looking over Johannesburg from the Carlton Centre

is unlikely.

A game ranger in the Eastern Transvaal described to me how he had seen a mamba rear up and strike a rhinocerus which had blundered over it. He said it was a very big mamba, about ten feet long, and it hit the rhino right between his front legs. The rhino walked on 100 yards or so, then his legs began to wobble, he stopped and fell forward on his nose, and when the ranger walked up to him he was dead. Total time from bite to death: just over five minutes.

South Africans love snake stories, and the country is of course well supplied with snakes, both harmless and venomous. A very typical series of South African conversations for men over the brandy and Coca-Cola, starts off with an account of everybody's favourite horror encounter with some terrible reptile, or nest of them. They will tell you about their little nephew of two who had a pet cobra at the bottom of the garden which he used to feed until his dad found it and shot it just in time, or the rinkals in the tree above their sleeping-bag, the puff-adder on the floor of the unlighted outside lavatory, the mamba in the rafters of the beach cottage . . .

Generally they will have ended its days with a heroic and accurate shot, though in fact if you knew them better you would probably find that the garden boy had killed it for them with a broom.

Then from the snake stories, with a few appreciative shudders and another good swig at the brandy, they will move on to tell you of the ferocity of their dogs. Many white South Africans love to have fierce dogs, to protect them. Those who find such comforts necessary will therefore tell you, at length, how ferocious their dog is and how he can tell when somebody is an African.

Then, when this topic has been exhausted and everybody has had a chance to tell about his particular Alsatian, Doberman Pinscher or bull terrier, there will be a pause for another stiff brandy or so, and the mood will become really sentimental and confiding, and the men will move on to their most intimate and tender concern – their relationship with their motor-car.

They will tell you lovingly, of its speed, its economy, its little ailments and how they were cured, and describe a performance which would certainly astound the manufacturers. Their children may have ceased to obey them and turned to drink and drugs, their wives may have gone off with other men, but at the end of the day they always have one thing to fall back on – their motor-cars love them.

6 The Karroo

'You ask the station-master at Kruidfontein Station, he's not a bad old bitch.' Oom Awie Muller speaking. Gnarled, sun-dried, leathery, very kind – even willing to try and talk English to a small boy from the city being sent off with the horse-cart on an errand to the station six miles away.

His wife was called Baby, and she told us once that she believed in washing her hair regularly, every year. In between whiles she rubbed castor oil into it from time to time. Awie spent a lot of time out on the veld.

He was a farm foreman, and he ran a farm of 5,000 morgen, which is 10,550 acres and was enough to carry 1,000 sheep in that sparse and arid landscape, the Karroo. When he took over the job the fences were all in disrepair – all seven miles of them. So on his first day he set out early in the morning carrying a basket of tools and spare bits, and that night when he came back the job was finished and the fences were all right again. I don't think his tools included any pliers, because his hands were tougher and more useful for the same job. At a *braaivleis* he would carry round, on the palm of his hand, a glowing wood ember for people to light their cigarettes from. He had not met many city folk and he was always delighted at their amazement.

The main national road, the N9, runs right through the middle of that farm which Awie use to run, midway between Kruidfontein and Leeu-Gamka, which was for a long time called Fraserburg Road before reverting to its more ancient name. Kruidfontein itself is named after the sulphur springs which bubble stinkily to the surface on the farm nearby, leaving a thick white deposit (not yellow as you might expect from sulphur) all along the edge of the rotten-egg-smelling stream it makes.

If you walk on into the scrubland you will find it very lonely and silent, and as you cross a few low hills and the road disappears and its sounds fade away and you hear nothing but your own footsteps and the occasional zing of a beetle in a thorn-tree, you might begin to think about travellers' tales of strange, huge beasts which they say have been sighted in these parts. Or on the other hand, you might prefer not to.

You will cross riverbeds, and you may find your progress hampered by the sand. It rains about four inches a year here, and sometimes not for three or four years at a stretch, so that most of the time the rivers have sand and dust in them but not water unless you dig. Then you will also come across little ruined shacks where Hottentots or very poor white farmers lived a long time ago – nobody remembers them now. You will, after an hour or so of walking, probably come up with a herd of black-faced sheep with fat tails, known as 'Persians' here, because that's where their ancestors came from, or thick-woolled Merinos, once jealously preserved in Spain and smuggled out for breeding elsewhere only at the risk of execution – (the Spaniards wanted the buyers of the best wool to have to come to them.) All of them will be busily nibbling away at what appear to be the lifeless, dried twigs of dead bushes – but they are Karroo bushes, and as the botanists will tell you, they are in fact very much alive. They need about five acres each for permanent grazing hereabouts, and they keep on the move. They are mostly untended, and the farmer may not see them for weeks on end himself, though if he knows his business he will certainly see to it that a shepherd or an intelligent youngster is sent off to look them over every few days.

On this farm, Awie's old farm, there are windmills scattered about all over, pumping water from deep boreholes into round concrete dams, to be tapped off carefully through a ball valve for the animals to drink. In the middle of the winter that water sometimes freezes an inch thick during the night, but during the day the temperature climbs up rapidly again, until by midday it is stinging hot.

When Awie's boss took the farm over in the 1940's, there were all sorts of ancient vehicles standing about, like Hupmobile cars and Diamond T trucks, which had given up hope during the depression of the 30's and stopped running.

They got them all running again with much oily improvising, cursing, banging and bolting, and towed them into life behind a more recent farm truck with excited yells of 'daar gaan hy' (there he goes') from everybody on the farm when the engines finally spluttered into life.

Later an old man called Mr Visser who was a brilliant mechanic and had had, somewhere in his past, a fine education, came to stay in a single room attached to the barn on the farm, and earned his keep and no doubt a little pocket money keeping all the antiquated machinery going. He had worked, as a young man, with the early x-ray equipment, he said, and his hands shook perpetually, but he repaired any machine that needed it, meticulously, and people knew of him and his ability for many miles around.

Kruidfontein station doesn't actually have a station as such, but there are some water-tanks and signalling equipment and sometimes a train stops there and you climb up into it from ground level and the station-master, who is a nice man as Awie said, might help you up with your bags. Near Kruidfontein station there are some superb vineyards, though most people would not believe that grapes could grow in such a place. They were planted by a small, wiry farmer called Mr Neethling, who wore glasses and a perpetual quizzical smile. He got them to grow by pumping great quantities of water up from underground from a very strong borehole, and irrigating them regularly, and he grew delicious grapes and made excellent wine from them as well.

The trader at Kruidfontein was for very many years a man called Bennie Franks, who found time to be a substantial farmer in his own right as well as running his stores. Like many Jews who have settled at such outposts throughout South Africa, he spoke perfect Afrikaans and was well liked by his Afrikaans neighbours.

Then, just along the road between Kruidfontein and Prince Albert there is J.D's place – a big farm from which J.D. makes periodic forays into Cape Town, where he wheels and deals and develops property, buys and sells and makes a fortune, though he always comes back to his real home out here in the almost-desert.

Just outside Leeu-Gamka the bridge crosses an important Karroo River formed by the confluence of the Leeuw and the Gamka. You can tell it's a big river by the clouds of sand which the wind blows up from it. It is a poor place from which to hitch-hike. Charlie Bloomberg, the South African writer, once tried to hitch a lift north from that point. He stood there, screwing up his eyes against the sand from the river, and every five or six hours a car or truck would be heard droning towards him, the first faint promising buzz growing gradually to a brisk roar as it finally zoomed past him.

On the second day he got a large packing-case from the storekeeper at Leeu-Gamka – it was called Fraserburg Road in those days – and in between the approach of a car or truck Charlie sheltered from the sun and sand in his packing-case by the side of the road. That night he slept in it. By the third day he was getting very unshaven-looking, and there was lots of sand in his hair and dust on his face and even some bits of karroo bush sticking to his clothing, he says. Also, he was getting tired and full of despair, so that when the cars and trucks came up he would wait in his packing-case until the last moment and then leap out and wave his arms at them. But they swerved to the other side of the road and then carried on, going a bit faster. On the fourth day, luckily for Charlie, an almost totally blind truck driver mistook him for a signpost and stopped to get a closer look at him, and Charlie was able to talk him into giving him a lift.

Of course most of the Karroo lies well off the highway.

Indeed, one little settlement hidden in the Swartberg Mountains and known as Die Hel (The Abyss), had no road of any description for at least 100 years and was reached by donkey-tracks through the mountain gorges until 1963, when a precipitous mountain road was finally pushed through. The Hel (it's not the devilish kind, though it sounds like it) is well-known in South African folklore as a 'forgotten valley' where the dozen or so farming families who had settled there some time in the past were so isolated that they even spoke their own variant of Dutch, instead of modern Afrikaans. They used to make their own clothes and live an almost totally self-sufficient existence, emerging once every year or so to make the journey through the mountains to Prince Albert, to trade wild honey and raisins for necessities like coffee and tobacco which they could not produce themselves.

There is a very curious little place at Matjiesfontein, still in this part of the Karroo, where the train used to stop for food and the local landowner built himself a little town like a Scottish crofters' village, dominated by a fine big ghostly hotel, with a tremendous collection of mounted animals' heads on the walls of its dining-room. It became ghostly because the trains stopped stopping there and the road was built to pass a few miles away, but it's well worth a little detour to see. Now developed, it is a major tourist attraction.

Pushing on north you will get to the main town in this part of the Karroo, Beaufort West, which has several hotels, a motel, a biggish dam, a Boer War fort built for British soldiers to guard the railway bridge against Boer guerrillas – you will see them all along the line – and is generally a well-established town. If your car is about to break down, arrange for it to happen here – you will have a better chance of getting spares and servicing for it than in one of the smaller places, though some of these small garages in the farming areas are well practised in improvising and getting a vehicle back on the road again, regardless of whether they have the proper spares or not.

Beaufort West is also famous for producing Professor Christian Barnard, who performed the world's first successful heart transplant.

From here on the distances stretch out between towns and you are advised to fill your petrol tank at each town, in case the pumps are closed for the night when you reach the next one. Any of these places is worth stopping at and spending time, but you have to think in terms of spending weeks or preferably months, to really start appreciating the life that goes on in these apparently deadly little 'dorps.'

E mornings in the Karroo will not take you a lifetime to discover however, just one experience should dó it. Whether you stay over at a hotel or – preferably – on a farm, get up at about five o'clock in the morning, winter or summer, and just walk about. The dawn breaking over the Karroo veld is a sight worth travelling far to see. There is a special quality of almost electrifying crispness in the still morning air, you can hear the sounds of a farmyard clearly from a mile away and the world seems suddenly very clean and full of promise, wherever you have been and whatever you have seen before you came here.

When you get to Colesberg it is also worth turning off the main highway and spending a day in the small town. It lies among a group of little hills, kopjies – pronounced koppies – and has a slightly wild-west air going back to the days when it was indeed quite a rough frontier town, with as much trading in gun-powder and strong drink as there was in wool or cattle hides. Nowadays it has an international reputation as a centre for breeding race-horses, and breeders like Dennis Silcock of the Knoffelfontein Stud have co-owners of some of their more spectacularly valuable horses living as far afield as London and Portugal, and they occasionally arrive from the world's great centres at little Colesberg to have a look at their four-footed investments.

The horses are so valuable that Dennis Silcock, for example, finds it pays him to employ people to wander through the thousands of acres where the horses are turned out in the veld, to pick up every single piece of dung, so that it can be carried back to the farm and burnt, to prevent parasites being transmitted this way. If he could find somebody to take the dung away, he'd be delighted not to have to burn it – but it's 500 miles either way to the rose gardens of Cape Town and Johannesburg.

The time to try and be in Colesberg, or any Karroo town like it, is when they are holding an auction of livestock, because this is the main social function as well as the main business occasion, and even for a townsman the restrained excitement of the farmers transmits itself. Surface appearances are, as always in South Africa, particularly misleading in these parts and that leathery old yokel in a greasy felt hat and stained trousers, champing toothlessly on an ancient pipe, may in fact be worth a million.

Some of them have been around, and travelled far from this quiet little country town. There is more than one Afrikaans-speaking farmer here who can also speak Italian – learnt from Italian partisans during World War Two. But generally they talk about sheep and horses, and sometimes cattle.

The Karroo itself used to be much more fertile, has been overgrazed by sheep during the last 100 years, and may again be reclaimed and improved and brought back to its former fertility, if the government persists with a controversial scheme for saving it. Farmers who were born there 50 or 60 years ago will tell you that when they were children it was much greener and had a much greater variety of self-seeded grasses and shrubs. But, as happened in Scotland and many other places, unenlightened farming practices which 'mined' the soil instead of farming it, killed off delicately-balanced natural species and eventually launched the whole vast area on the downward slope towards a ruined dustbowl, exactly as happened in some of the Western parts of the United States of America earlier this century. But the authorities have woken up in recent years to the ruination of the land and an ambitious programme for saving the Karroo has been launched. In very broad terms, it involves paying farmers compensation to let certain areas of land lie fallow for a number of years, to give nature a chance to heal the wounds.

There has been agro-political controversy about it and the scheme has tended to surge ahead in times of prosperity and then be pruned right back again when the country was passing through one of its recurrent periods of economic slackness, so the overall success or otherwise of the project continues to be debatable. Certainly, however, one can meet farmers in the Karroo who will tell you that some little streams on their own farms are flowing again for the first time in living memory, after several years of keeping the sheep off the land and leaving it to recover, and that areas which they knew as sand pans or scrub areas on which nothing grew, are now green again and that birds are coming back to nest there. So while grave mistakes have been made in the past all is not lost and, as President Brand of the Free State once expressed it, 'all will come right if every man does his work.' It has come to be the unofficial South African motto, and tells us a lot about the people, but they generally only quote the first four words.

It is very important to the country's future that the Karroo should be saved, because it is part of a vast semi-desert area which occupies by far the greater part of South Africa and which is steadily advancing towards the east, in some parts at the rate of half a mile a year. When people talk vaguely about the natural beauties of South Africa and its natural wealth, they often overlook the fact that most of the country consists of 'badlands', in which people can scrape a living from a ruthless bony landscape only with great perseverance and a stoic acceptance of drought and year long blinding heat.

To get a rough idea of just how huge a proportion of the country does consist of this scorched 'badland', take a map of South Africa and a pencil. You can start at the top western point of the country, at Alexander Bay on the Skeleton Coast, and go right down to Saldanha Bay to mark the first salient of the really dry, hot part of the country. Then from there you can draw your pencil across to De Doorns in the Western Cape, to Montagu, Oudtshoorn, Willowmore, Somerset East, and then North via Cradock, Burgersdorp up to Kimberley and beyond that straight up north to the border at Mafeking. Then you can complete the map of the hard lands with a line right along the entire northern border of the country, from Mafeking westwards until you reach the Atlantic Ocean, and all the way it will be dry and the land, most of the time and in most of the places, will be burnt red and the grass where there is any, will be the colour of dried straw. You will have marked out an area about the size of France, and by far the greater part of South Africa, and there will be a great many hot, dry places which you have left out, though of course you will also have included a few green and fertile valleys and successful irrigation areas and fine farms with plentiful water.

To grasp something of the essential national character both of the land and its people, you have to sit for a while and contemplate the nature of vast, hot, dry, largely empty spaces and the effects they have on people who are familiar with them. Toughness, surely, in every sense, must be one of the characteristics which such places will produce in people, as well as hospitality and a keen interest in the occasional strangers who find their way there. Also a certain suspicion and fear of a remote, unreal 'outside world'. In this connection one has to recall that television only started to arrive in South Africa in the mid 1970's, so that people living in these isolated places can have had little to help them form any extensive visual picture of what the rest of the world looked like, or the people in it.

If one wonders, as a newcomer, how on earth anybody would wish to remain in a place like, say, Pofadder or Sutherland, one finds that quite often the people there are asking themselves exactly the same question, and there is a constant movement out of them and away towards the lush, green places towards the east, and to the bigger towns and cities. One has to remember that this arid west was not nearly so arid a century or so ago, and nor were the towns and cities big enough in those days to provide as much of a pull as they do now. And then, to be fair to them, those little towns do have a more compact, relatively cosier social life of their own, where individuals are known to each other almost from birth and have an established place in their society which big cities do not offer.

7 The Orange Free State

The Orange Free State is by far the most Afrikaans of the four provinces, just as Natal is said to be 'very English'.

Most of the people in it are, of course, black, but for more than a century the Whites have run it, and nearly all of them have been Afrikaans, giving it a very distinctive quality. Dutch Reformed puritanism is a strong influence – indeed, many of the towns were started off by the church arranging the sites and forming the first organs of local government, through its elders and church councils.

Sundays, therefore are observed with great strictness; to a Calvinist or other strong seventh-day-observance believer, Sunday in the Free State must seem very satisfactorily quiet and dignified, with almost everything except church services either locked up or forbidden – including fishing and playing football. To an outsider they seem terrifyingly grim and boring.

The dreaded 'outside world' has as little impact here as the authorities can manage, and foreign ideas of liberalism are much resisted. Not long ago a British immigrant school-teacher in Bloemfontein was sacked for explaining to his pupils the significance of the international peace sign – although the authorities did comment that this was not the sole cause for his dismissal, but 'the last straw'.

For Africans in this society the rules are particularly clear and strict. They can remain in their tribal areas, or they can come into the white areas to work for the white man – preferably on his farms. When they have finished their useful working life they are 'redundant Bantu' and must return to their tribal areas, where they may die at their own leisure.

Until very recently a siren could be heard every night at nine p.m. in Free State towns – the warning to all Africans to be off the roads and back in their 'locations' or in the hut-like rooms which they occupy in the back yards of their white masters' houses.

For many years Indians were not allowed into the Orange Free State, even in transit by road between the Cape and the Transvaal, except for one or two trading families who apparently got in before the prohibition and stayed on, by special dispensation, quietly running their shops and keeping their heads down.

In gaining dominance in this area the Boer settlers were not only tough, persistent and self-confident – qualities you will still find well represented in the Free State – but they were also fortunate in their timing, in that the Africans who occupied this part of the country were passing through a period of tremendous tribal chaos at much the same time as the first settlers were elbowing their way in among them.

What happened was that the Zulus launched a great wave of military terrorism on their neighbours, shattering and destroying other tribes in what was known as the wars of the Difaqane, from about 1822 to 1836. The effects of the attacks launched by the successive Zulu warlords – first Dingiswayo, then Shaka, and later Dingaan with other warrior chiefs like Matiwane and Zwide joining in – were that the tribes were ravaged and pillaged over a vast area. This extended from what is today the Eastern Cape, over the whole of Natal, the Free State, the Transvaal and right across the Limpopo into Rhodesia, where the Matabele, fleeing their Zulu cousins, in turn conquered and came to dominate the indigenous peoples.

None of this was directly due to the presence or arrival of the white man on the scene, but it must have been very useful, when one was with some difficulty buying and leasing land among tribesmen, if those tribesmen and their chiefs became weak and scattered at the same time due to events going on in their own society.

Whole tribes were massacred, cattle and huts were

abandoned, crops left standing or unsown, while the people fled the ruthless impis (Zulu armies) with their stabbing spears, or those other armed men who were in turn fleeing before the impis themselves.

There was desperate famine and there was even, eventually, widespread cannibalism. There are many bizarre tales of cannibal practices from this period. An Anglican clergyman for example, whose diary I found in an African homestead in Basutoland, was working from the 1840's in that region which was one of the worst-hit areas, where the refugees came over the Drakensburg mountain ranges to escape the Zulus and he recounted numerous incidents of cannibalism which he had heard of. One women told him, years later, how she was captured together with a group of other women and children washing by a river, and dragged away by tribesmen to their own village: when they reached the village the villagers greeted them with excited yells of 'Food!' and they were kept bound up in a hut and taken out and eaten one at a time. She survived because she was very pretty and one of the cannibals wanted her for a wife.

Some of the tales are reminiscent of half remembered European legends, perhaps dating back to similar times in western history, like the story the same clergyman tells of the treacherous warrier chief who agreed to guard the grain supplies of a tribe, kept on top of a large flat-topped hill which could only be approached through a single narrow cleft, easily defensible. Having got the grain up onto the hill they jeered at the tribesmen, refused to give them any of the grain and sat on top of the hill eating it for months, getting fat while the tribesman starved.

Eventually the cheated tribesmen went and fetched a band of cannibals, exciting them with tales of the fatness of the warriors on the hill. They were, apparently, so tired of eating thin, starving people that they thought it worthwhile to climb up the sheer sides of the hill under cover of night. The story had a happy ending – for some: the cannibals ate the fat warriors and were so grateful for the feast that they returned the grain to the tribesmen who had brought them there.

When one comes to trace out how places like the Free State became as they are today, one finds an awareness of this sort of sombre background built into current attitudes. If the Whites seem to be, on the whole, rather contemptuous of the Blacks, they are liable to point to periods of barbarity and chaos in black society, which they have seen virtually happening around them, and to argue that they are better off under their leadership. You are likely to hear this type of argument stated more often and more forcefully in the Free State than anywhere else in South Africa.

But, as always in South Africa, there is another side to the story, and there are many examples of kindness and care for the lesser privileged in this ultra paternalistic society.

A few years ago the Free State's neighbour, over-populated, poverty-stricken but independent Lesotho, suffered a particularly bad drought and there was widespread hunger. The people became so exhausted and the farmers so undernourished that it seemed unlikely that many of them would even have the strength left to prepare their lands for the next season's crops, even if the rains did come.

Quite spontaneously, a large number of Free State farmers stepped in at this point, organized themselves into a peaceful commando, as it were, and suddenly arrived on the border of Lesotho in a huge convoy of trucks, tractors and their beloved 'bakkies' (small, fast, open pick-up trucks), loaded with ploughs, fuel, supplies and equipment.

They crossed into Lesotho and proceeded to plough thousands of acres of the Basutos' arable lands for them, so that all they had to do was go straight on to planting their crops without the arduous work of ploughing with their oxen and single-furrow ploughs.

There is a long-standing claim by the neighbouring kingdom of Lesotho, which used to be Basutoland, to a large part of the Free State which Lesotho says should be part of itself. Again, this dates back to the period of disorganization among the local tribesmen, towards the middle of the last century while the Whites were establishing a new state for themselves in the area.

10 Jo'burg. The Strijdom Tower at night

There was a brief period, from 1848, during which the British annexed the area between the Orange and Vaal Rivers. One of the objects of this exercise was to establish and keep the peace between the Whites settling in the area and the Africans and Griquas, (considerable people at the time, of mixed Hottentot, White and African origin.) The Griquas were themselves relative newcomers to the area, having been pushed northward in front of the advancing white settlers.

H. Lichtenstein, writing in 1806 (*Travels in Southern Africa in the Years 1803, 1804, 1805*) describes how families of mixed Hottentot and White blood, who often assumed the name of the White family for whom they worked, had first come to establish themselves on small properties towards the Sack river, but:

> when the increasing population of the colony occasioned new researches to be made after lands capable of cultivation, the white children of the colonists did not hesitate to make use of the right of the strongest and to drive their half yellow relations out of the places where they had fixed their abodes. These Bastard Hottentots were then obliged to seek an asylum in more remote parts, till at length, driven from the Sack river, as they had been before from the Bokkeveld, nothing remained for them but to retreat to the Orange River.

Thus they found themselves among the contenders for living space in what was to become the Free State. In 1843 their chief, Adam Kok, (together with other chiefs, including Moshesh of the Basuto) signed a treaty putting him under British protection, but the Boers did not recognise these chiefs as having acquired any special authority, since they did not regard the British as having legitimate sway over the area in the first place.

There was quite a serious fight when Adam Kok, supported by 100 of his armed followers, tried to arrest a Boer farmer for flogging two of his coloured servants. The Boers raised a commando to fight back and eventually the British governor, Lieutenant-General Maitland, sent in troops on the side of the Griquas, who with this support defeated the Boers at

11 Durban. A street in the Indian quarter
12 Durban. Surfing at South Beach

Zwartkoppies.

So it was a turbulent part of the country in the middle of the last century and when the British annexed it in 1848 one may imagine that most of the Boer inhabitants received the proclamation with jeers rather than cheers.

Before very long some of the exceedingly tough and independent-minded farmers, particularly from the Winburg area, decided to throw the British out and called for help from fellow-Boers in the Transvaal. Their commandos were routed, but the British were tired of this turbulent possession and in 1854 they handed over independence at the Bloemfontein Convention, creating the Orange Free State Republic.

The leader of the most powerful African tribe in the area, Chief Moshesh, who was indeed the founder of the present state of Lesotho, believed that his boundary with the new republic was that established in 1843 in his treaty with the British; the Boers later disputed this, and although a boundary was finally agreed in 1864 when the president of the Free State called in the British Governor of the Cape Colony to mediate, the people of Lesotho continue to argue from time to time that much of their rightful land lies within the Orange Free State, as it is now.

Winburg, the Free State's oldest town, where the sturdily-independent farmers came from, is today a quiet little town around a large square and has a population of about 5,000, of whom the 1,500 Whites occupy the central part of the town.

It got its name, incidentally, not from any victory at a ferocious battle, but when the founding Voortrekkers who were trying to decide on a site for it in 1835, finally picked on a particular farm and the jubilant owner called it 'Wenburg' because he had defeated his neighbours who wanted the honour for their farms. Later it came to be spelt Winburg. It is very much a small agricultural town and as such very typical of the Free State, surrounded by great plains with big farms on which the main crops are usually maize, or wheat grown in fields which often extend over hundreds of acres.

There are cattle ranches, some sheep farms, and many of them have a few horses, though of course these no longer play the part in farm life that they once did. But the Boer nomadic herdsmen rode, hunted and fought on their horses, so the animal holds an honourable role in Afrikaner folk memories, and Afrikaans farmers like their sons to be good horsemen, though they would seldom bother with such English activities as show-jumping or formal hunts.

Some Free State farmers have discovered that it is more profitable to dispense with exotic animals like sheep, which have to be dipped and doctored to keep them alive in hostile Africa, and to put the country's indigenous animals to work earning money on ranches where they used to roam in gigantic herds. Thus there are numbers of them who have springbok instead of sheep, for example.

Springbok, the country's emblematic animal, can jump very well indeed as their name implies, so springbok farmers have to put up fences getting on for ten feet high. But once they have got their herd established on suitable grazing land, there is not much maintenance to do since the springbok are adapted by nature to survive and thrive in these conditions; to crop them the 'game farmers' merely have to allow eager hunters to come and shoot a certain number of them each year at so much a head.

Throughout the country, but particularly in the Free State and Transvaal, there are game farms where most of the native antelopes are reared – or encouraged to rear themselves. It is one of the most interesting developments that the country's farmers have yet tackled and some of them are very skilled with the animals they have on their farms and ranches, even to the point of being able to handle safely such potentially dangerous animals as eland and zebra.

There are of course state-run 'game parks' dotted all over South Africa, and the Free State has a particularly attractive one around the Allemanskraal Dam, known as the Willem Pretorius Game Reserve. It is well stocked with representatives of the original highveld wildlife such as springbok, zebra, hartebeest, blesbuck, wildebeests, the very gracious and beautiful impala and the fearsome-looking but comparatively docile white rhinoceros.

There are also some interesting relics of the former inhabitants of this area on the Doringberg heights near the dam, where a vanished tribe built thousands of stone huts, each just big enough for one person, as well as cattle kraals, also from stone.

The most attractively-situated town in the Free State is Parys, which lies on the south bank of the Vaal River, with its broad, calm waters ideal for boating, swimming and fishing and with numerous islands stretching out in the middle. It is a remarkable contrast to cruise along the Vaal in a boat and see the almost continuous row of luxurious holiday homes stretching along the Transvaal bank, while on the Free State bank there is hardly any development at all. It reflects the different levels of prosperity in the adjoining provinces and also a different approach to life altogether, the Transvaal being bold, entrepreneurial and expansive, the Free State cautious and conservative. Those who are interested in real estate and holiday homes will be fascinated by the Transvaal bank with its holiday cottages, boathouses and holiday mansions, but those who prefer natural surroundings left largely to themselves will prefer the Free State side.

Parys, in any case, is a well-developed little town of some 15,000 people offering good facilities for travellers and holiday makers to enjoy the river, as well as being a thriving agricultural centre.

The great physical characteristic of the Free State is spaciousness – great tracts of open veld with its knee-high grass, dry and straw-coloured for most of the year but briefly green during the rains, interspersed with scattered bush, thorn and acacia trees and from time to time a great cultivated field, usually with maize, wheat or sunflowers growing in it almost as far as the eye can see, or freshly ploughed and awaiting the next crop.

Most South Africans have a great fondness for 'the veld', and like to drive through it, walk about in it, look at it, and think about it when they are elsewhere. The Karroo is too daunting for most, with its expanses of naked laterite, gravel, sand and stone with an occasional stunted bush or thorn-tree.

The very lush green of the Western Cape and the Eastern coast strip is so small in comparison to the rest of the country as to be quite uncharacteristic, but the open veld and bushveld is the most familiar of all South African landscapes, and as close to the nation's heart as 'Sarie Marais' *braaivleises* and rugby.

Towards the eastern end of the Free State, on the road along the edge of Lesotho near Natal, one passes among some very spectacular sandstone cliffs and peaks known as the Golden Gates, and there is a branch off the main national road which goes through the Golden Gates National Park – high, lonely hills quite well stocked with wild-life, with great swooping vistas which will make you feel either bigger and better or small and frightened, depending on the size of your soul!

The most important city in the Free State is of course Bloemfontein, and it is certainly worth a stopover for anybody interested in this large, paradoxical province – open to look at but closed in so many ways.

Bloemfontein is the judicial capital of South Africa and the country's judiciary has a well-earned and much-respected reputation for impartiality.

This must take professionalism and courage well beyond anything which the job would require in most other Western countries, bearing in mind that the Court of Appeal itself lies in the heartland of Afrikanerdom, where Calvinist attitudes impart to governments a Godly righteousness which they would never dare claim in Western Europe or the Americas, for example. The upper echelons of the judiciary are themselves often recruited from leading Afrikaner families, so that when their judicial decisions at the court of final appeal go against government policy – as they sometimes have done – they may well be subjected to accusations from relatives and old friends, of cultural and political disloyalty. There is no evidence that this deters them from doing their duty as they see it, and one should reflect on this.

Bloemfontein is a clean, light, airy, modern city with a particularly sunny climate. Being a modern city it is rather lacking in interesting architectural features – but if one expects the modern capital of a ranching province in a hot country to look like Venice, then one is creating one's own disappointment in advance – just like South Africans who go abroad and complain that the English countryside does not resemble that of the Free State.

T. V. Bulpin, in his highly readable and useful *Discovering Southern Africa* (particularly recommended to travellers by road) has an engaging account of the founding of Bloemfontein. The area was known to the Africans, he tells us, by the much more dramatic name of Mangaung – The Place of the Leopards. He tells us that:

> The first known European to settle there was Johannes Brits, in 1840. He built a simple homestead and started to farm. Six years later, in March 1846, the surprised old farmer was startled to see a group of horsemen and wagons approaching the veld.
>
> In the van of this party rode an officer of the Cape Mounted Rifles, Major H. D. Warden, seconded to the responsibility of being official British Resident on the Central Plains of South Africa.
>
> Major Warden was something of a romantic figure. The son of an illegitimate offspring of one of the over-arduous Stuart princes and an Edinburgh beauty, Warden had, early in his life become a professional soldier. Now here he was, far from the elegance of Princes Street, Edinburgh, riding across the veld searching for a suitable site for his residency.

He bought the farm from farmer Brits for £37. 10s, 'Brits and his somewhat bemused family moved off to a new farm,' and Warden founded Bloemfontein. As a town it obviously caught on, though as we have seen the British handed it over to the Boers a few years later, in 1854. It has one of the country's leading private schools, Grey College, and a university. It has its share of museums and monuments, including a very large obelisk to Emily Hobhouse, an Englishwoman who tried to help Boer women and children suffering in British concentration camps during the later, 'scorched earth' stages of the Anglo-Boer war.

For campers there is a particularly pleasant resort about 18 miles out of Bloemfontein, called Mazelspoort (Measles Pass – Measles was quite a scourge in the nineteenth century) where there are boating as well as good camping facilities. Bloemfonteiners often take their leisure there.

If you are sympathetic, or benevolently neutral, in your response to Calvinism and the way of life it creates, then you will agree with the description of quiet, healthy, well-disciplined Bloemfontein by many who know it as, 'a good place to bring up children.'

8 Johannesburg

'Inindaba wena fikili lapa?' 'Why did you come here?' I once asked a young Mshangaan tribesman far underground in a Reef gold mine, in the 'Fanakalo' kitchen-Zulu spoken in the mines. 'Mena funile buga Johannesburg,' he said, 'I wanted to see Johannesburg.' It is the city with the greatest pull south of Cairo.

Hard, gritty, rich, ugly, fast, set on the topmost ridges of the highveld 6,000 feet above sea level, more days of sunshine than California, freezing cold in winter while the sun shines on regardless, winter air like iced champagne. There is only one real reason to be in Johannesburg – because that's where the money is, and only one real reason why the money is there – because that's where the gold is. What's left of it, that is.

The mine dumps stretch all along the southern edge of Johannesburg's main city centre, and they go on stretching out from east to west for something like a hundred miles, from the old mines around Springs in the east to the new ones in the Free State. That's a lot of gold. But most of it has been taken out already and the Reef mines might have another 25 years left in them.

Will the party come to a sudden end when they go? South Africans argue about it all the time. It could well be the main industrial city of Africa by then, so Johannesburg will not automatically close down the last head-gear stops turning.

Meanwhile many of them are still spinning at a good rate, dropping cage-loads of men down when at 30 miles an hour, 6-10,000 feet below the ground, where it's so hot that the air has to be refrigerated before it is pumped down and the pressure of the world above you is so great that now and then a chunk of rock just pops out of the floor or the wall or the ceiling – what miners ominously call the 'hanging wall'.

You can only see the mine dumps and the head-gears, and mine-dumps are, after all, what's left when the action is over, so they give a misleading impression of tranquility. Under them there is a whole world going on, with hundreds of thousands of men working like demons in the bowels of the earth – drilling into the rock with jumper drills driven by compressed air, that bounce as they spin, making a noise like a machine-gun in a locked room spurting out a jet of water at the same time to lay the deadly silicosis dust that would otherwise turn a man's lungs to cement in six months – and used to, in the old days. Charging up the holes with sticks of dynamite, priming them with a 'doppie' (detonator) at the end of a length of fuse that fizzes as it burns, spluttering out drops of tar and an acrid smoke. Lighting more fuses, very quickly, with a 'cheesa stick' (literally, a 'hot stick') made from compressed gunpowder, that will go on burning fiercely even if water from the hanging wall pours down over it as you are lighting the charges, because it is very important that they should all go off after they have been lit. Many a good man has been killed by drilling into a misfire. It is also important that you move out after the charges have been lit, and nobody needs any urging about that, although sometimes there are mistakes.

Miners get paid on Friday and sometimes whoop it up half the night before going down early on Saturday morning, at about five o'clock, so as to come up again early for the week-end. The most pock-marked man I ever met was one of those. He said that when he went down on the Saturday morning he was still drunk, so he handed everything over to his boss-boy (African foreman, who sometimes seems to know more about mining than the mine captain himself) and went and sat on his box in a quiet tunnel for a highly illegal sleep. He woke up a few hours later with a great start, all by himself in dead silence – no drills going in the distance. In panic and confusion he thought that they must have finished the day's work and somehow gone off and left him underground without completing the day's blast, so he rushed straight into the workings to see what was happening. Only when he was right in the middle of a stope – the open space, maybe 150 feet wide, 200 feet long and three feet high which is left as they take out the layers of gold-bearing ore – did he hear the fizzing and smell the burning fuses. It was too late to run back, he said, and he just had time to drop into a crouched-up ball against the footwall (floor) with his hands over his eyes, when the first blast went off, on his right side. He was far enough away from the blast not to be killed, but the flying smaller rock debris hit him like half-a-dozen simultaneous shotgun blasts all along his right side.

A second later he got it from his left. He managed, somehow, to stay conscious and staggered and scrambled out of the stope to be rescued by his 'boys,' who had come back to look for him, themselves risking being gassed by the nitrous fumes from the dynamite blast (it is an interesting form of gassing – it doesn't kill you straight away but eight hours later your lungs suddenly fill up with fluid and you drown).

Each side of him, including the sides of his face which his hands and arms could not cover, looked like mincemeat, and the pockmarks it left on his face were truly spectacular. 'The girls never liked me much before,' he said wryly, 'but after this I said to myself, 'Christ, my boy, now you can really forget about it.'

At the beginning of each shift the miners go in to see what their blast of the previous day has achieved, the white overseer going in first in case it is dangerous (in theory, though rarely in practice).

Then they 'bar' out with a crowbar the bits of rock that are broken but not quite loose, 'lash' away the shattered gold-ore and waste rock with shovels, load it into 'ngolovans' (little steel trolleys on rails) and 'tram' it away to be dumped into an ore-shute, to be hoisted up in giant buckets called skips for final crushing and processing on the surface. A ton of rock may after all this yield a quantity of gold about as big as the tip of your little finger – but if it's more than two pennyweights a ton, it's still worth it.

There is usually a bonus system underground, from the 'machine boys' who work the jumper drills upwards. Those 'machine boys' push their heavy drills, spinning, bouncing and roaring, into the rock for eight hours at a shift, sometimes lying on their back and pushing with their feet, sometimes with their assistants, the 'spanner boy', bracing his back against theirs for extra force. The muscles they develop will make you look twice before you believe it. They often plug their ears and sometimes smoke marijuana to deaden the effects of their working conditions, and they get paid a bonus for everything they drill above a certain minimum daily target. So they do not like to be interrupted in their work and they are generally treated with a measure of respect, and indeed caution.

In fact the relations between Whites and Blacks underground in the mines are generally more pleasant and cordial than any I have seen on the surface in this tense country where the few exploit the many. There seem to be many reasons for this – everybody's job is very clearly defined, the circumstances are extremely rough and potentially dangerous, and you either pull together or die together, so to speak, and considerable cameraderie exists.

On the surface the white miners tend to live either in mine accommodation – mine captains and managers get houses at minimal rents, often with tennis courts, and swimming pools, because they have to live on the job – or in white working-class areas, where they are usually conspicuous by their smart motor-cars, being rather better paid than most working men and needing to show it somehow.

The Blacks are mostly tribesmen from neighbouring territories. (Black South Africans prefer not to work underground in mines, especially if they can get better-paid and less dangerous work in industry.) They live in mine compounds in very basic concrete barracks with a minimum of privacy and living space, but plenty of good food. Sociologists complain about it, because the men are away from their families for a year or 18 months at a time and the conditions are said to be unnatural. There is a certain amount of homosexuality, and low-grade prostitutes hang about the vicinity of the compounds, but the mine authorities try to provide various facilities to keep the men happy in their leisure time, and they do not seem to dislike compound life on the whole. Most of them have football grounds, they organise their own tribal dancing and music (an absolute must for any visitor to Johannesburg, the mine dances on a Sunday), some of them cook local tribal dishes to sell to homesick fellow-tribesmen in the compound on days off, and they also arrange huge stick-fights and other gladiatorial displays, sometimes attended by thousands, on neighbouring mine-dumps – violent occasions sporadically frowned on by the authorities.

As a group, the black miners of Witwatersrand are probably the strongest and healthiest working men in the entire continent. A mine doctor told me that it is not uncommon for them, coming from a malnourished tribal background, to put on 40 pounds weight in their first six months, with the combination of extremely hard physical work and large, balanced meals provided by the mines with, of course, good medical care.

One of the leisure activities taught is knitting, and it is a curious sight to see large, muscular black miners sitting about doing their knitting in the compounds or even at football matches.

The Blacks in the mines have also, for very many years, been grossly underpaid by international mining standards, (although there have been recent pay increases). The authorities have basically two answers to this: firstly, they say that if they paid them proper miner's wages, comparable to overseas countries, they could not afford to run the mines, and secondly they point out that the men come from places like Mocambique, where there is virtually no cash-earning employment available for them, and that they have no alternative jobs.

Meanwhile, 'lapa pezulu' (up on top) live the people who are getting the real benefit of the activity carried on at the pace and with almost the same risk as a war, way beneath their feet and, many of them feel, their notice.

If you go up to 'The Wilds', quite a large section of original kopjie painstakingly developed into a really superb informal African hill garden on the ridge to the north of the city centre, you will look north across mile after mile of solid affluence. Swimming pools, well-tended gardens, highly polished motor cars, deferential Black servants in spotless white, tennis courts, a continual round of parties – cocktail parties, bridge parties, dinner parties, barmitzvah parties, Christmas parties, New Year parties, going away parties, coming back parties, Sunday morning sherry parties, Sunday lunch time *braaivleis* parties – any excuse for a party. The only party that is never held in these fat, opulent suburbs is a Thursday night party. Thursday is the maid's night off.

'I would ask you back for something to eat at my place,' says the Johannesburg hostess, 'but of course it's Thursday.' She grins deprecatingly and turns up her hands and raises her eyebrows. You all grin, nod several times and turn your hands out, palms upmost. You all understand. You all have the same problem. Thursday is the maid's night off.

In Johannesburg the contrast between rich and poor is most evident. The Blacks do the dirty work, and are exceedingly poor. The Whites make the money and are exceedingly rich. They spend it with a certain desperation, with the air of a man who marvels at his amazing good fortune, and enjoys it as fast as he can, knowing that soon somebody may tap him on the shoulder and enquire: 'Just a minute – where did you get all that?'

The feeling of guilt is thick in the air, and also of indignation at 'the outside world,' 'the overseas press,' 'liberal agitators,' 'communists,' 'trouble-makers,' and anybody else insensitive enough to apply the tap on the shoulder and launch the dreaded enquiry: 'just where did you get all that?'

Perspiring slightly they launch into a sort of catechism of South African Newspeak; 'It's not cheap labour at all really, you think they have low pay – for them it's a fortune – you don't realise what a low standard of living they have, actually they wouldn't want this house at all, they really wouldn't want it', 'many of them dress better than we do, what do they need money for? They've got everything, we give them everything – work, a place to sleep, clothes, food, pocket money, good hospitals – I wish I could have so few worries,' and the rest of it.

If they are Christians, they will explain that they are not anti-Semitic at all, really, but the only thing they have against the Jews, they will tell you, 'is that they pay the servants too much and spoil them for the rest of us.' They will say this unsmilingly, with a sort of innocent cynicism.

Their ostentatious enjoyment of their wealth, too, has a certain childlike innocence about it; chandeliers in the kitchen, one might call it. The boasting is done in the form of complaints so as not to appear too obvious; 'Have you got any idea what they charged just the four of us for only two weeks skiing in Switzerland? . . .'

Of course not all white South Africans are rich. Indeed, if you are accustomed to the motherly care of the British Welfare State you will be shocked to see the number of derelict whites lurching around places like Johannesburg. Life is much tougher here and professional layabouts tend to go hungry. For Whites in the cities there are social welfare services but they need to be in really dire straits before they qualify for any hand-outs.

Blacks who have no money and no work eat poorly, if at all and there is a great deal of malnutrition among them.

Vast tracts of basic housing for the Blacks stretch for mile after mile into the veld, well outside Johannesburg. The streets are on the grid pattern, the houses tiny cottages with a yard or so of front garden, often lovingly tended. Compared to the opulent white suburbs a few miles away they are heart-breaking. But compared to the slums around most of the other cities in black Africa they are very good housing indeed, and compared to the high-rise blocks of flats built for poor people in Britain, America and parts of Europe, they are quite reasonable places to live in.

Certainly, the black suburbs, or 'locations' of Johannesburg have their grim aspects – lack of street lighting, gangs of murderous 'tsotsis' (young thugs), lack of waterborne sewage and supplies of electricity. But they are at least basically serviced, policed and planned. There are schools, churches, sports fields and social centres and most of the people who live in them manage to bring up their families in tolerable comfort and health.

In judging them, one is up against the double set of values which always applies to South Africa and makes things so hard to evaluate: it is a Western society planted in Africa – do you judge it by Western or African standards – what comparisons are legitimate and fair?

Not all Whites are rich enough to have chandeliers in their kitchens, of course, or to boast about holidays in Switzerland, but one mentions these people because although they can also be met in the rest of the world there are more of them, proportionately, here and they are more vociferous, more tolerated and less mocked, their brash self-confidence largely unshaken by the social changes that have been altering values in the rest of the western world for a decade.

Most of the white people here, around Johannesburg, are ordinary hard-working folk not much different from people you might meet around any fair-sized city in Britain or America. Their way of life is on the whole more like that of the Americans than the British, because their standard of living is about the same as that of Americans. The main differences are that they enjoy an excellent climate and therefore spend much time out of doors, and that the majority have domestic servants who do most of the chores around the house, which frees the white housewife either to do a job or to enjoy the benefits – and problems – of a great deal of leisure at home.

The city itself is particularly hard and brash to look at. It started out as a mining camp in the 1880's and was laid out quickly, efficiently and without imagination. The buildings are starkly modern – they tend to be pulled down and replaced with something bigger after about 30 years. The great mine dumps to the south of the city centre are impressive and grand in their way – even beautiful – but they also give off great quantities of fine dust which blows about and penetrates everything when the wind is up. However, a new strain of grass was eventually developed to bind the dumps, which are being landscaped. The average day in Johannesburg is bright and sunny, not too windy. In general, the rain falls in summer, and it falls in the afternoons – extremely hard, with a few great big drops at first, so hefty that they strike up dust as they hit the ground, and then a deluge when it falls in sheets. If you walk through 15 seconds of this downpour you will be soaked to the skin. But if you stay under cover for a bit the downpour will cease just as suddenly as it started – one minute, the kind of deluge that made Noah take to his ark, the next, a sudden silence like the switching off of a great tap, the hot sun comes out again, the rainwater swirls away muddily down the drains and runnels, and the steam rises from the ground.

Winter is really cold – a biting, penetrating, freezing cold that will raise chilblains on your hands if you don't wear gloves, although the sun is probably shining at the same time.

People from the northern hemisphere tend to think that they could never have too much sunshine, but in fact the unrelenting, blinding, blazing sunshine of Johannesburg can become extremely exhausting and depressing. It is not that it is excessively hot – days when it is over 90°F are exceptional – but just that it is so monotonous. Almost every day of the year, the glaring sunshine beating down on the arid landscape, the grass parched almost permanently yellow, the rocks sticking up through the thin, red, sandy soil. It is a place to wear dark glasses, all the time.

Being a new city it has all the standard facilities of a modern machine for living, and some of them are very good. South Africans are particularly keen on ballet and not only do the main international companies like the Royal Ballet in London have a high number of South African dancers, but good dancing may be seen in the country itself, and Johannesburg is well to the fore in this tradition.

There are also several professional theatres in Johannesburg, and international stars frequently visit the city for a run of a few days or a week or so. There is much live music, including concerts of a very high standard. There is

13 Karroo landscape near Muringspoort Pass, Cape

14 A Transkei African with Execution Rock in the background

also African jazz of a high creative level, though inaccessible to Whites. Top Johannesburg live entertainment could be classed as of international standard.

Cinema however, is heavily censored. Sex generally is officially frowned on by the Afrikaner moralists who run the government, and for this and a complex of other reasons it has a special flavour of forbidden excitement in this wealthy, over-leisured city.

Other facilities are, on the whole, good. Food is slightly cheaper and more generously available than in Europe, though the standard of cooking is often not good. Liquor is, broadly speaking, about on the price level of France rather than Britain or the United States, and Johannesburgers are great drinkers. The pubs, however, tend to be all-male establishments and the few which do open their doors to women are very recent and women who go into them unaccompanied are likely to be subjected to heavy male overtures. Libraries are very good. Parks are scarce but well-run. Museums are worth seeing because of their unique collections from the country's own rich historical background. Johannesburg's art gallery is unfortunately situated, just overlooking the main railway station, but has many impressive exhibits reasonably well displayed.

In commercial art galleries it is not uncommon to find the works of such major artists as Salvador Dali, priced from about £6000 upwards, and selling well.

There are many sports clubs, well patronized and playing a major role in the life of so prosperous and sunny an outdoor city.

Doctors are private and good; for some reason South African dentists are especially good and their work is admired by dentists in other countries. The Johannesburg general hospital enjoys a sort of rota system whereby the city's leading specialists give a certain amount of their time each week, either free or for nominal fees, and poor white people can get the best treatment for whatever they can afford, or less. Black people have the Baragwanath Hospital, which is also said to be very well equipped and staffed, though often overloaded;

15 Kokerbome in the North West Cape

16 Looking down the river valley of Port St John to The Heads with the highest number of traumatic deaths in the world per thousand people per day to cope with, most of them Black.

South Africans, White as well as Black, are very keen on violence, battering, murdering and killing each other in various ways – particularly with motor cars – at a spectacular rate, statistics published in Pretoria make it quite clear that South Africa in general, and Johannesburg in particular, is well up around the top of the world league when it comes to violence. It is just as well, therefore, that they have good medical services.

Johannesburg is a hard-working, generally very efficient city and if you have the money to pay for it you can usually expect good service and good value.

Advertising is often brash and even fraudulent, a situation which would not be legally tolerated in most Western countries. There are of course excellent advertising companies doing work which would stand up anywhere in the world, but they work in an atmosphere in which it is permissible to advertise motor-car tyres as being 'safe at a hundred and sixty', cigarettes as being essential to your virility, and patent medicines as being able to cure cancer.

Most businessmen in Johannesburg are honest and are keen to have professional associations and codes which will enforce their honesty, but there are plenty of others too, and some of them are extremely rich. For example, retreading dangerous tyres for African motorists is a favourite racket of fringe businessmen. The reputable firms will tell the motorist that the ruined tyre he wants retreaded should be thrown away. Being very poor, and also ignorant, he will hawk it around until he finds one of the unscrupulous operators who will retread it for him. Which of them is to blame when it blows out on the road?

But the majority of the population are quite ordinary people who are not dishonest, or particularly violent, and many of them are fine people, well worth knowing. They live in a particularly strange society, surrounded by problems not of their own creating and one must bear this in mind when meeting them.

Among the man-made canyons of this great ugly city there are plenty of city characters who spend their whole lives walking on tarmac, surrounded by concrete, and playing the many variants of the game of survival in the city. Most of them are respectable, solid citizens whose games take place within the rules, but some of them make their own.

Ziggie the Greek, for example, a handsome if slightly cadaverous young man, lived comfortably for years off a set of x-ray plates showing a pair of tuberculosis-riddled lungs. He got the plates from a girl-friend who was a nurse, and he showed them to the Jewish Board of Deputies and convinced them that the plates were his own and that he, a good Jewish boy, was slowly dying of his illness and ought to have a monthly pension to live on meanwhile. They looked after him generously for quite a few years until somebody finally pointed out that not only was Ziggie Greek Orthodox, rather than Jewish, but also that his lungs were in excellent shape, the donor of the original plates having died long since.

'Peaches', was known to many customers of the two coffee-houses which he frequented as a leading lawyer. (Coffee-houses is a bit grand, really – they are 'Greek cafes', ubiquitous in the Transvaal, generally run by Cypriots or Greeks and serving very useful multiple functions. They combine the role of the American drugstore for youngsters and others to hang about over tea, coffee or milkshakes, and the British transport cafe. One can get a quick basic grill there in one of the permutations of steak, eggs, chops, chips, beans, tomatoes, toast, and from about seven in the morning till midnight they sell bread, milk, cigarettes, newspapers and a range of other essentials.)

'Peaches' favours two of them in particular, one in Hillbrow and one closer to the city centre, and holds court there almost every evening, giving learned opinions on current *causes célèbres* before the courts, well spiced with inside information about the participants and informal quotes from the opposing counsels, garnered apparently in the robing-rooms and judges' chambers. Impressed, many a fellow coffee-drinker brings him a little legal matter to sort out informally, and

Peaches gives judgement and technical advice, charging nothing but graciously allowing his interlocutor to pick up the tab for his steak-egg-and-chips. It is only those who know him very well who also know that his legal knowledge comes entirely from his habit of spending most of the day dozing in the spectators' benches of the Supreme Court.

Johnnie Sprague was an entertainer, and made up in confidence what he lacked in expertise. He once put on a magic show in a small Transvaal town in which, with the assistance of his girl-friend, every single trick in the entire act misfired disastrously. She handed him the wrong bucket and he got drenched while the stage caught fire; she mixed up the watches and he smashed up a genuine gold watch instead of the cheap one; she put the blindfold on so that he couldn't see at all and he fell into the orchestra pit in the Houdini act – but as one disaster succeeded another the audience cheered and roared for more.

Finally, drenched, burned, ragged and nearly exhausted, Johnnie held up a top hat and shouted: 'and now, for my last great act of the evening I am going to produce, from this hat, without any tricks or illusions, a fully-grown bull elephant weighing fifteen tons.' At this point the cinema manager, who had never lost faith in Johnnie's magic for a moment, brought the house down by rushing down the aisle screaming passionately: 'you're not putting any bloody bull elephant on that bloody stage – it'll go right through the floor!'

9 Transvaal Country Towns

After Johannesburg comes Pretoria, which is only 38 miles from Johannesburg but so different that it could almost be in another country altogether. Johannesburg is stark, ugly, rich, commercial, fast, bright, flashy and polyglot. Pretoria is gracious, staid, good-looking, peaceful, dignified, moderate and Afrikaans.

Pretoria is 1000 feet lower in altitude, which makes it considerably hotter than Johannesburg, and people have paw-paws growing in their gardens. Some white people live in ordinary, comfortable suburban houses with front gardens and back yards right in the middle of Pretoria, although in the city centre such houses are now somewhat outnumbered and over-shadowed by tall new buildings, hotels and blocks of flats. But it is a city that has quite visibly been planned, its development organised with a certain stateliness befitting the nation's administrative capital. The Government head offices are all here, although once a year the Government packs itself onto a special train with all its top aides, secretaries and files, and departs to spend the legislative season in Cape Town, leaving Pretoria even quieter than usual.

There are handsome squares with fine buildings dominating them, the avenues of jacaranda trees deserve their fame, and the seat of Government, Union Buildings, looking down on its many acres of elegant formal gardens and expanses of lawn, is a pleasure to see.

The feeling of the city and its way of life is dominated by the presence of the Government and the Afrikaans majority. One's impressions are of a certain air of decency and of reticence. The streets seem to be full of huge, muscular, sunburnt schoolchildren in khaki and policemen. There is very little crime. Indeed, one feels that unlike the hectic streets of Johannesburg this healthy, scrubbed, antiseptic atmosphere would be singularly unproductive of any sort of criminal activity.

The reticence is peculiarly South African and proceeds from a strictly hierarchical system in which opinions may only be entertained by the man at the top, and information must also come only from the top. There is a great fear among underlings of saying the wrong thing, and this becomes almost pathological in their relations with unknown writers and journalists. At first, coming up against this constant refusal to say anything, other than to refer one to the Minister, one tends to suspect that they must be hiding something. On closer investigation one discovers that all they are hiding is their normal working lives, conducted on the whole in a straightforward and efficient manner.

The ultra-defensiveness, however, relates to the fact that as a government they have been under unremitting attack for a quarter of a century, not only from overseas writers, but almost daily from a surprisingly courageous and outspoken opposition press.

They are attacked, of course, for their Apartheid policy and the various unhappy consequences which it has for a great many black South Africans. They are hardly ever praised for its occasional beneficial results, or for their other numerous completely non-Apartheid achievements. They have therefore, long ago, decided to 'go into laager' symbolically hunched inside a ring of their sacred ox-wagons, peering out over the sights of their Mausers as the hostile tribes surge and howl outside.

If you are interested in gathering information from them beyond what is instantly available through official sources, then they prefer you to prove yourself 'reliable' and not to misuse their confidence. It can make for a tense atmosphere and some absurd results, and people who know both cities often say that the official atmosphere in Pretoria is very much like that of Moscow.

As a young reporter I was once trying to check a report that a drought in the Western Transvaal had at long last been broken by heavy rain. We had no contacts in the area and the only person we could get on the telephone was a policeman in the police station at one of the outlying towns in this arid area. Could he confirm that they had had rain? There was a long suspicious silence and finally he said: 'no sir, I'm afraid I am not authorised to tell you anything.'

This intensely cautious attitude can be counter-productive. Near Pretoria there is a major new African settlement called Garankuwa where a large township has been laid out for about 15,000 people, many of them working in factories between Garankuwa and Pretoria. Visits to such Bantu areas by Whites require a special permit issued only in Pretoria, the officials explained to me at the entrance. They were polite, even friendly and apologetic, but quite firm. 'If you want to have a look around inside and meet people who live there, first get your permit,' In due course, a written application for the permit was refused, without explanation.

I made enquiries from a number of people who lived in Garankuwa and some who ran businesses there. Without exception they confirmed what I had already heard elsewhere: the place is a model township, they have no complaints worth mentioning, they are delighted to be living there. Authority, it appears, is sternly hiding away one of its best success stories.

But this 'laager' mentality is changing quite fast and Prime Minister John Vorster has for many years made overtures to various African states in an outward policy of developing friendly relations with any Black African state that will accept them.

This outward-looking policy has had some visible consequences in Pretoria itself, with black businessmen and diplomats from other countries being accepted at the city's best hotels. They can be seen happily lunching there, frequently as the guests of South African Government officials. Black South Africans are also admitted – but only if they are dignitaries from the Homelands, which have a status about halfway to that of foreign countries, thus partially exempting their citizens from racial laws.

However, it is not evident from a glance whether black Africans come from Homelands, friendly African countries, or just outside Pretoria, and it would be embarrassing and the source of potential diplomatic controversy if hoteliers had to ask black guests to produce their credentials to establish what type of black people they were, so various black South Africans have from time to time joined the other diners in these luxurious precincts, and nothing has been said. As long as nothing is said, the Apartheid rules and regulations can quite safely be ignored at many points. But it will take some time to dismantle them officially.

Pretoria has some quite outstanding facilities, institutions and amenities. The work of Onderstepoort Veterinary Laboratories is known world-wide and will no doubt play an increasingly important role in agriculture for the whole continent. The Council for Scientific and Industrial Research has some first-class brains working with plenty of resources at their disposal – but again, in conditions of exaggerated secrecy and caution which prevent much of their work getting the attention it deserves. The Bureau of Standards is one of the best-equipped in the world.

The Pretoria zoo is remarkable for its imaginative landscaping. The lions are kept on a big expanse of hillside in conditions very similar to their natural habitat and humans who want to look at them can walk through their enclosure, protected by a caged-in walk, so that in this section, at least, one sees a rather desirable reversal of the usual roles – the people being in the cages and the animals in the open.

The hippos have their own lake, the birds have splendid aviaries and it is all spread out in a most beautiful and extensive landscaped garden, a very pleasant place to visit. Some of the animals are still kept in the traditional old-fashioned small cages, but experts on zoological management are impressed by the handling which they receive. There are veritable armies of African workers and attendants to be seen, and both they and their white supervisors are encouraged to form friendly relationships with the animals they handle, which not only makes the animals easier to handle but also, apparently, keeps them much happier.

The university, like most other things in Pretoria, is also well-conceived, clean, large and shapely. It is 'traditional' in its outlook and tends not to encourage students to criticize their elders.

This is not to say, of course, that there are not some outstandingly brilliant individuals among both faculty and students, and in this quiet and orderly atmosphere (students wear short haircuts and official university uniforms to public occasions) they can get on with their work and do from time to time produce impressive results.

Potchefstroom, another Afrikaans town, demonstrates to a still further degree the effects of a strict adherence to Calvinism and an old-fashioned Germanic view of the sacred nature of authority – the direct line through parent to Head of State to God. Until quite recently Darwin's thoery of evolution was not officially countenanced at Potchefstroom, other than as an example of a religious heresy. But 'Potch', as it is called, is nevertheless a sweetly sleepy little town, with an engagingly seedy character and the students there are also nice and clean, as in Pretoria.

Another Transvaal university is Turfloop, which is for Blacks from the Homelands of Bophuthatswana, Venda, Gazankulu and Lebowa – each one of them a new state as big as a small European country, with a combined population of about $4\frac{1}{2}$ million. The university town here will be Seshego – a new capital still to be completed, and meanwhile the nearest town is Pietersburg. All the Bantu universities are controversial, because they are the apex of the system of Bantu education, which is not only separate from White education, but also different. Those who design it and run it argue that it is a practical system of training people, mainly through their native language, in skills which will actually be useful to them, such as agricultural methods and other largely manual skills, rather than educating them in a tradition of Western thought which will not help them in their lives. Those who oppose the system claim that it is a deliberate means of retarding the development of the black people of the country, systematically fitting them only to perpetuate their roles as workers for the Whites and they call it 'education for slavery. Both have elaborate arguments and evidence to support their case.

Again, if one is really interested, the best method of finding out is to go to a university like Turfloop and get talking to the students. This might be frowned on officially, and even attract the attention of the Special Branch, depending on how loudly you talk and what you say. Students who have not met you before will not, in any case, generally talk very frankly because they have their careers to consider; there have been troubles at all these universities, and troublemakers are likely to find themselves eased out – or just kicked out. Turfloop is modern, bright, spacious and designed with an imaginative blending of new building systems and African motifs.

In one of the biggest student strikes which they have had there in recent years the authorities did not call out truckloads of armed white riot police, let alone the Saracen armoured cars kept for crowd control in emergencies – they merely called in an African police officer and asked him to handle it, and he did, with considerable tact, and there was no violence or intimidation on either side. It seems that the South African authorities, too, are learning.

The towns of the Transvaal offer a great spread of climatic character, from the dry bushveld places like Zeerust on the edge of Botswana to the west, though the lush lands along the banks of the Limpopo, across the great plains of yellow grass down to the hot, humid sub-tropical valleys of the Eastern Transvaal.

Oom Willem – we shall call him that – lives in the great western bushveld, about 30 miles from the iron-mining town of Thabazimbi (The Mountain of Iron – the Africans knew about it a long time ago). His farm is so big that, having entered his front gate, you drive for about 20 minutes on a good straight gravel road before reaching his farmhouse. His servants come out at once and remove your luggage, wash the dust off your car, show you in, make you a cup of coffee, whether Oom Willem, a widower, is there at the moment or not.

Up till a few years ago, he says, he used to be worried by that distant blue mountain on the horizon. 'Eventually,' he says, 'I managed to buy it, and now I own everything as far as I can see in any direction, so I think my farm is now big enough.'

His great joy is his prize Afrikander cattle. He has thousands of cattle, but the best of them he has bred and fed and tended to a stage where they must be among the finest humped longhorns in the world, and he has the trophies to prove it. 'They have gone beyond the point where I could ever get their value back as slaughter cattle,' he says, standing among half a dozen bullocks bulging and glistening with well-being, 'but I'll explain why I do it with a little story.' (Illustrating a point with a homely little parable is a favourite Afrikaans gambit): it appears that there was once a cockerel, living on a farm in the bushveld, who went scratching around some distance from the farmyard one day and came across an ostrich egg in the bush. He hurried back, fetched all his hens and paraded them up to the monster egg. 'Now girls,' he addressed them, 'I want you to take a good look at that. It's not that I'm trying to make you feel bad or anything – it's just that I want you to see what can be done'.

Oom Willem has had no European company for some years now, since he lost his wife, but his Africans look after him and he looks after them, he explains. Just before dinner we find him in his study, talking over farming matters with half a dozen of his African workers. Several of them were born on the farm, most of them have been with him for at least a generation, each of them has his own special responsibility and his opinion is listened to very carefully, though Oom Willem takes the final decisions. Oom Willem sits in his easy-chair, the Africans are in a semi-kneeling position. resting one knee on the ground to show respect for his age and seniority.

They seem quite comfortable and the talk is animated. He has a drink in his hand but they do not: he will give them a drink later, but he will not drink with them – it is not the custom. If a visitor, introduced to the servants, extends a hand to shake theirs they will fold their arms and back away, nodding and smiling politely for it is not the custom on this farm to greet a white man with a handshake.

After dinner the headman sends a message through the cook that he and his friends have made a nice fire outside and would be glad if Oom Willem would join them with his friends.

They have built a blazing hot fire – bushveld nights are cold – protected from the wind by a tightly-woven 'skerm' of dried branches, gnarled, twisted and grey like driftwood and artfully worked together so that they form a solid wall against the wind on three sides. They have placed little carved stools for the white visitors and they once more assume the one-knee-on-the-ground position, or squat comfortably on their hunkers. They seldom see visitors here and they are anxious to know as much as possible about us but they put their questions with a certain grace, avoiding direct personal questions if possible; it is a pleasant evening.

Oom Willem pays them top rates for the area, gives them a generous allowance of beef and maizemeal and provides working clothes. They build their own huts. If they want their children to go to school he gives them a bicycle to ride to the nearest one, and pays the fees and buys their books. If they get sick he takes them to hospital or sends for the doctor, who charges £20 a visit because of the mileage. Anything he wants done he asks for and it is done with great enthusiasm. Anything his workmen and their families want from him, they ask for and he generally gives it to them. As far as it goes – and it certainly covers his life and theirs – it seems to suit both parties.

But the carefully-observed 'customs' about not touching Whites are not local tribal customs: a few miles away, across the Botswana border, members of the same tribe will greet a white visitor with a handshake, or a hearty slap on the back if he is a particular friend. They will look him straight in the eye when they speak, and will sit down on a chair in his company or stand at the bar next to him and drink with him, with neither legal nor customary barriers. On Oom Willem's farm they observe the 'customs' which belong to the old gentleman's tribe, if not theirs, because they know that's the way he likes it.

Between Johannesburg and Pretoria, on a large ranch with a private airstrip, lives Uncle Tommy, who makes his living developing townships and selling them and likes to go diamond prospecting in wild country when he wants a change, and also likes a drink. He lives by himself, with his servants, who pinch a goodly share of his food and drink but look after him very well just the same.

After a two-day drinking bout Uncle Tommy toddles out into the sunshine in his khaki shorts and bare feet and goes to inspect the workshops, walking straight into a pool of oil. 'Come out of that,' says his black chauffeur kindly but firmly like a good nanny, 'just look at your feet, you're getting oil all over them,' and he takes Uncle Tommy by the hand and leads him out of the oil, but declines the invitation to join him in a drink – he feels it might be embarrassing when Uncle Tommy is sober again.

Jonas, the old gardener, who walked to South Africa from Malawi many years ago, sleeping in trees to avoid the lions, and then worked in the mines for 30 years before being kicked out as unfit through silicosis, lives here illegally, because since he is officially too old to work he is classed as a 'redundant Bantu' and is supposed to go back to where he came from.

Jonas has as many stories as Uncle Tommy himself, and he also loves a drink, so he joins Uncle Tommy in a session, but he keeps one knee on the floor as he does so, because that is how he learned the custom in this country and he would feel uneasy drinking with his boss any other way. But they drink and cackle together nevertheless.

In the middle of the afternoon two more drinkers arrive by small private plane. They circle over Uncle Tommy's house several times, one of them hanging out waving a bottle. He seems to be the navigator. Uncle Tommy rushes out, waves, cheers and falls into the fish-pond. His friends make a very bumpy landing on the airstrip. Another session is under way at Uncle Tommy's. When he is not drinking, Uncle Tommy spends more time helping other people than doing anything else and he is known and liked for 20 miles around, though perhaps not altogether approved of.

Most of the smaller towns in the Transvaal have a distinctly prosperous appearance and look as if their main centres had been freshly rebuilt this century – and indeed that is often the case, if they have not just been built for the first time.

But some of them have been there for a relatively long time – more than 100 years is a long time in Transvaal history – and have settled down most attractively into their surrounding landscape. One of my favourites among these is Barberton, which started off with a roar of excitement when Fred Barber and his mates struck gold there in 1884. It is difficult to imagine now that this tranquil little town at the foot of the mountains was a wild rip-roaring mining town before Johannesburg was even thought of – not long before, but still Barberton did get there first. Prospectors, adventurers, miners, investors, hawkers, trollops, all came rushing and the town sprang up overnight.

Perhaps fortunately for Barberton the gold ran out quite soon after a few years of spectacular discoveries, otherwise it might have grown into just another of the world's great concrete jungles like Johannesburg, instead of settling down into a charming town of a comfortable size, big enough for a person to be known among the other townsfolk.

It lies in a particularly lovely sub-tropical valley, reached by road from Nelspruit, and known originally by the frightening name of the Valley of Death. Today, in lush surroundings of well-ordered farms growing mangoes, sugar-cane, and avocado pears, with tangles of flowering plants by the roadside, one cannot see the point of such a name, but of course for the first white men who struggled through these valleys the malaria mosquito lay in wait and to a mosquito, as Archie said to Mehitabel, 'a human being is just something to eat.'

All that is changed now, the mosquitoes have largely gone and you should get no malaria as long as you take your anti-malaria pill once a week as it says on the box (please read the instructions carefully – a friend of mine died not from malaria, but from taking the once-a-week pill once-a-day).

Barberton, like Pretoria, has jacaranda trees but a more genial, less worried and purposeful atmosphere. It is not only hot here but humid, and it generally seems about time for a drink, and people generally seem to be having one. They get on with their work, but not as if they had to get rich very quick just before dropping dead, as in Johannesburg, or to keep up with the work at all costs lest the country should fall apart, as in Pretoria. They just get on with it in an amiable way, and this is the case throughout these delightful little towns of the Eastern Transvaal – Sabie, White River, Pilgrim's Rest, take your pick, they are all pleasant and set in great valleys, progressively farmed and ambitiously forested.

Sabie, indeed, lies in the greatest man-made forest in the world, run by that same enthusiastic Forestry Department which looks after the ones around Knysna in the Cape.

For somebody with a week off I would say that this is the part of the Transvaal which most repays a wandering visit. There are excellent camping facilities at many points – although in recent years companies that manufacture caravans have taken over many of the best camping sites and forbidden the traditional South African tent there, because they want people to buy their caravans – a form of progress, no doubt.

Sabie also had a gold-mining past, and its mining lasted much longer than Barberton's; the mine here starting in 1880 and only giving out in 1950. Nearby is one of the more romantic of the ghost towns which once were mining villages – Pilgrim's Rest. It is carefully preserved largely in its original form, and worth a visit all to itself, any time.

All over this area and into Swaziland there are the remains of mines, many of them little one-man affairs, where one can step from the surface straight into the worked-out stopes (and go on falling straight down, if you're not careful) where millions of pounds' worth of gold was taken out in the great days. There were even highwaymen to waylay the gold coaches on their way to Pretoria – and it was not that long ago; one of them, Hutchinson, married several African women in between robbing the stage-coaches and one of his grandsons, of a more peaceful and literary disposition than his grandpa, went to Britain and became the senior English master at a Brighton school.

One can arrange a large, rambling, circular drive starting off, preferably, from Barberton and then going through Nelspruit and Sabie, allowing a day for a visit to the Sudwala Caves overlooking the Crocodile River.

These huge caves have not yet been fully explored. At one stage they belonged to the Swazi people – Sudwala was a famous headman – and the Swazis used to hide in them when their relatives, the Zulus, were in a particularly warlike frame of mind. They are as spectacular as the Cango Caves in the Cape.

The grand circular tour of the Eastern Transvaal, of which there are several interesting variants possible, ought to take in the canyon of the Blyde River and then to go on via Duiwelskloof through Magoeba's Kloof to rejoin the main north road at Pietersburg. The journey passes great hills, giant valleys, huge forests, waterfalls, charming towns – wonderful countryside.

In the Magoebaskloof valley you are in the country of the Rain Queen, Queen Mujaji, who is said to have inspired Rider Haggard to write *She,* and tribesmen say that she is immortal. She came to this valley about 400 years ago – she must have been quite a young woman at the time – bringing with her not only her followers, but the rain as well, which falls most plentifully here, due to her magic. She is much respected by other tribes, who send tributary gifts when they want her to intercede and get some rain for them as well. She is also shrouded in mystery, surrounded by very loyal protectors and her harem of attractive young men, and most definitely not available for viewing by the casual tourist.

Also in this neighbourhood, not far from Pietersburg, lives another extraordinary African figure – the great religious leader who heads the Church of Zion, the biggest Christian sect in the Transvaal and probably the country and who lives in his own town, marked out as 'City of Zion' in white stones on the hillside above it. He does not welcome non-church members and there is a notice on his private road saying: 'no journalists or policemen allowed here.' It is not only the Whites who have authority.

Every year, at Easter, tens of thousands of the followers of this highly colourful church converge on their leader's private city and to move among them on that occasion is to experience one of the great durbars of Africa – this time a religious durbar with the sound of hymns rising up constantly among the beating of drums, skirling of flutes, intricate rhythmic music from African xylophones, the sound of the ankle-rattles worn by dancers, and even bagpipes. The leader himself moves about in considerable state. At one stage he had a Daimler which was originally brought out to South Africa in 1947 for use by the King and Queen of England on a royal tour, and he travelled about in that with his uniformed footmen riding on the running-boards.

As an act of devotion, each follower brings either a goat or its equivalent value in cash to the gathering, and I have seen attendants carry out 17 large metal washtubs laden with silver coins at one gathering, the notes being removed in suitcases. The church ladies generally wear white robes and red or blue hats and sashes when they are going to church meetings. These are often held in the garages of white employers in the suburbs of Johannesburg, where the devout in their robes are a familiar sight. The menfolk wear similar robes on ceremonial occasions, but they also express their faith with a variety of costumes of their own design, some of them even wearing kilts, (somewhere along the line, the Scots have made their mark in Africa). Their gathering at the City of Zion is not of course intended as an entertainment for visitors, but if one can secure an invitation from a member of the church it is an experience in sheer creative, religious exuberance which is deeply moving in its own way, even for a stranger.

10 The Wildlife Parks

The Kruger Park is the biggest and best the country has, and by far the best-known. It lies in the lowland bushveld right against the eastern border of South Africa and Mocambique, and it is well-stocked, run on the most efficient and modern lines and its facilities for camping en route are indeed excellent – comfortable furnished rondavels (an adaptation of the traditional African beehive hut) with hot and cold water, freshly cut well-dried firewood for your *braaivleis* – everything spick and span, and an abundance of wildlife.

Paul Kruger, the great Boer leader, set aside the original land for Kruger Park in 1898 with admirable vision and foresight, and the people who have built it up and run it since then deserve nothing but praise. The site of the Kruger Park seems to have been chosen primarily because it was at the time the last considerable extent of land left more or less unfarmed in the Transvaal. As it happens, it lies in rather flat bushveld country where the characteristic vegetation is generally quite dense, so that the wildlife is not so easily observed as in the parks which have huge plains. The species which live there are of course those of the bushveld, and though these are well represented and fascinating enough for the ordinary visitor, the connoisseur of wildlife parks may well regret the absence of some of the species which the East African parks can show in great numbers.

Also, and this perhaps more particularly for the South African visitor, Kruger Park has developed such a well-earned reputation for excellence over the years that it tends to be overcrowded, and the regulation of these numbers and their safety requires many rules.

In earlier years South Africans earned a great reputation as wanton slaughterers of wildlife, and as a result there is much less wildlife left alive and at large than in most of the rest of Africa. But in recent generations they seem to be trying to atone for the sins of their forefathers by becoming outstanding conservationists. South African wildlife experts and conservationists are familiar, and usually welcome, figures at international scientific meetings, where they have much to contribute. Indeed, Ian Player, elder brother of the great golfer, Gary, has twice won the Conservationist of the Year award from the World Wildlife Society.

Starting at what seems to be the southern tip of the continent (in fact Cape Agulhas is) the Cape Peninsula has its own 30 square miles of Nature Reserve, a great pointed promontory with the Indian Ocean on one side and the Atlantic on the other, ending most dramatically in the Cape Point lighthouse, with a look-out point for visitors offering a terrifying view down onto the jagged rocks and great surging waves many hundreds of feet below. For dramatic and beautiful setting, this little reserve can certainly compete with anything in the world. It is unspoilt moorland lying between the cliffs, leading down to beaches and coves at many points.

To walk through this heathery aromatic scrub bush, with the little dark tarns lying concealed until you are right on them, preferably in a high wind roaring in from the sea, is one of the most exhilarating ways to spend a day that I know of.

There are eland, bontebok, blue wildebeest, springbok, zebra, ostriches and baboons roaming about in the reserve. Watch out for the baboons – they are very naughty and can be nasty if you get too close, especially if they are carrying babies at the time, which ride on their backs like miniature jockeys or cling on underneath their mothers' chests. They are keen on titbits from passing cars and one or two of them, a few years ago, had perfected the trick of ripping out the windsceens of parked cars to get extra titbits inside. I met a fisherman who got back to his car for lunch just in time to see a baboon proudly marching off with his lunch-tin in one hand and his coffee-flask in the other.

The South African dog-faced baboon, such as you find at Cape Point, is a formidable beast and although they are very intelligent and some people make pets of them, they must be treated with the greatest caution. In former years it was more common to find them as pets on farms and even in suburban households and there are many legends of their ability to learn. For many years there was a Karroo station master who used to ride about on a huge Harley-Davidson motor-bike with his baboon sitting on the pillion behind him, clinging on with its arms round his waist. They used to go drinking together in pubs and Karroo-dwellers who knew them will swear by everything that's holy that when the station-master got too drunk the baboon used to drive them both home on the motor-bike.

In the Cape Point Reserve plants as well as animals are protected, but one can go fishing from famous cliff-ledges such as Rooikrans, and even skin-diving for abalone (better known in South Africa by their Afrikaans name of perlemeen), which are particularly plentiful on the icy Atlantic side (maximum permited bag: five per person – enough for five delicious meals.)

Going up the Garden Route of the Eastern Cape heading towards Natal one finds a whole section of coastline maintained as a National Park on the Tzitzikama coast. The official brochure says: 'surely one of the most impressive seaboards in the world, with its lush green forests almost tumbling over the towering cliffs into the deep green waters and relentlessly thundering waves . . .'

It is, in fact, just like that, and there are great trailing lianas hanging from the forest trees, with monkeys swinging and screeching among them, forest shrubs and ferns and rare birds like the Knysna Loerie and the Narina Trogon. It is a coastal rain forest with giant yellow-wood trees (one of which is said to be 2,000 years old) and comes right down to the beaches, where there are cottages for visitors as well as good camping facilities. The marine life is partly protected here – you can fish in the conventional manner but if you go into the water with scuba equipment you must leave your spear-gun behind.

The best camping-place is at Storms River Mouth.

Further along this route, the Addo National Park near Port Elizabeth is also worth at least one day's visit. It is somewhat more than 18,000 acres of dense bush where the great attraction is the herd of about 50 Addo elephants, in a special 6,000-acre elephant pen of their own within the park. There is a perimeter road right round their camp and raised ramps for visitors to get a view of them, and if you still haven't spotted any from your car, then there are special feeding grounds where they come along by themselves, just below the park's restaurant.

The Addo Park has some rhinoceri, too – all in their own special camp, hippopotami and about 200 buffalo.

The buffalo look deceptively similar to cattle, peeping round the trees at one under their heavy horns, which look like old-fashioned men's haircuts parted severely in the middle. They are of course much better able to look after themselves than cattle ever could and the males have a special hooklike projection above and behind their rear hoof for stomping the life out of a fallen enemy after they have already tossed him with their horns. There are scarred and crippled hunters scattered all over Africa with tales to tell of how savage, crafty, and tenacious is the African buffalo. The Addo Park is one of the smaller, more specialised parks and in addition to the collection of elephants it also has a 1,200-acre section, well provided with roads, containing representatives of every antelope species indigenous to this area, the Eastern Cape.

Inland from Port Elizabeth, near Cradock, is the particularly interesting National Mountain Zebra Park, which was specially established to protect the most important remaining herd of this almost extinct animal – a dwarf zebra that stands only four feet high and is not found anywhere else in the world. The striping of this little animal is also different from that of its bigger, more well-known cousin. The stripes do not meet and they do not have the shadowing found in the other species.

There are camping and caravan sites in the park, which has a good collection of buck and is well-established as a refuge for wild birds – more than 140 species of them, right up to the ostrich. There are walks and rides through the mountains in the park, and footpaths to Bushman paintings. The Mountain Zebra Park also offers a unique farm museum, showing a South African farm of the last century with its typical housing, clothes, ox-waggons, horse-carts and carriages and an old water-mill.

Further east, Grahamstown has its own nature reserve – one of the country's newest, about 800 acres and already sporting a collection of white rhino, zebra, hartebeest, wildebeest and buffalo. Grahamstown is one of the cities more specially smiled on by nature, lying as it does among fertile, wooded hills within easy reach of the sea. Immigrants, particularly from England, are likely to find themselves very much at home here, with the added benefit of a superb climate.

The new reserve (The Thomas Baines Nature Reserve) incorporates the highly scenic Howieson's Poort reservoir, and is being developed with particular attention to its plants and filowers. Indeed, the aim is no lower than to become the Kirstenbosch of the Eastern Province, so that it is not only a superb amenity for the fortunate people of Grahamstown itself, but also a point to make for on any trip round South Africa. The city itself, with its fine old schools, its university, the special nostalgic atmosphere evoked by its many churches, museums and historic buildings is, next to Cape Town itself, probably the most charming in the country.

A lot further up the coast, Zululand has got 12 wildlife parks which are among the most exciting in the country, because this is where the visitor, accompanied by game guides, is allowed to get out of his vehicle and stalk the animals on foot, armed with his deadly 35 mm camera.

There are different terms for wildlife parks in South Africa: the National Parks are the main ones, run by the Government, next come the game reserves run by the provinces, and then the nature sanctuaries run by smaller local authorities or other organisations, and then a variety of private game parks, shooting ranches and wildlife farms.

Zululand has the Umfolozi Game Reserve, which has the world's greatest collection of white rhinoceros and the St Lucia Game Reserve which lies on a lagoon so wild and tropical that a sign warns the casual swimmer: 'These waters are infested by sharks, crocodiles and swordfish.' And if they do not get you, the hippos will. Then there is the Mkuzi Game Reserve and the Ndumu – one of the more remote ones, of special interest to the bird-watcher – and the national parks of Sordwana Bay and Kosi Bay further up the coast.

Zululand has of course a wild past, with much bloodshed. The Zulus themselves were mighty warriors, killing each other, their neighbours and the white intruders with equal efficiency and even wiping out a whole British regiment at the battle of Isandlwana. In the last century the hunters moved about slaughtering the animals until they had nearly exterminated some of the most interesting species, such as the white rhinoceros. Gradually the Zulus have been persuaded to adopt less warlike ways – for warriors they are an extraordinary good-natured people – the hunters have also been tamed and the surviving wildlife is now protected in the parks and reserves.

The Umfolozi Game Reserve became the last sanctuary for the white rhinoceros which was fast dying out. Today there are so many in this romantic, mountainous park with its two rivers, the Black and White Umfolozi, that the game rangers catch the surplus ones and export them. It is an amazing operation to watch. Travelling in a Land Rover with its doors off so that you can get in and out quickly and its windscreen wound down flat, you set off through the bush where the game scouts have spotted a likely candidate. Next to the driver rides a marksman with a specially-fitted rifle carrying a large hypodermic filled with tranquiliser. The terrain is extremely rugged – dense bush, thorn-trees, river-beds and dongas, rocks, sand and shale. Then suddenly through the bushes you see the rhino. He has seen cars before so he goes on munching while you edge the vehicle up as close as possible. His flight distance is about 50 yards and the effective range of the special gun is not much more than that, so this is the tricky bit. Just as the marksman is about to fire, the rhino decides the Land Rover is making him nervous and goes plunging off through a bush; the driver pushes his foot down, the vehicle bucks and crashes through the undergrowth, a great grey backside comes momentarily into view and – plaff! the rifleman has planted his dart. The ranger stops the vehicle, you all jump out and follow the animal on foot – rather cautiously, he may be irritated by now. He moves on forward through more bush, comes into a clearing, seems to be slowing down, stops, shakes his head from side to side and slowly slumps down. You close in on him at once and prop him up – his full-weight must not be allowed to rest on his lungs while he is unconscious.

The rhino's eyes are still open, so a ranger applies antiseptic eye-drops to keep them moist and protect them for the next few minutes. They do a quick check-over the huge body to see if he has any abrasions or recent damage that needs treatment, or any serious defect that would make him a bad prospect for travel. While this is going on a specially-designed truck has been backed into place. A heavy rope attached to a winch is brought out and fastened to the rhino rather like a horse's head collar.

Now comes the really ticklish part – giving the beast the shot of antidote to the tranquiliser which will wake him up, if we get it right, enough to walk groggily into the rhino-crate himself, but not enough to turn on the men who are handling him. The dose, this time, is exactly right. Within literally seconds of getting his second injection of the day, the rhino begins to get to his feet. The rope on his head tightens gently but firmly and begins to pull him into the crate. At the same time all the men lift and push him, patting him and urging him on 'come on, there's a good boy, in you go now, gently does it, there's a good lad . . .' just as if he were a dear old farm horse or cow instead of three tons of armour-plated danger. In he goes. The crate is lifted on – back-to-front so that if it stops suddenly the rhino's weight falls backwards harmlessly onto his behind and not forwards onto his neck. Off he goes, into a holding-yard and a penning system for several dozen fully-grown rhinos at a time – run as calmly and safely as any farmyard. The whole rhino-trucking operation has taken about as long as a farmer would need to catch a pig and put it in a trailer for the market.

The Umfolozi has lions, so the foot safari here has a certain added spice and must certainly not be undertaken without the guidance of the professionals. (These game-rangers, by the way, in their smart uniforms and dashing Land Rovers, work hard and long in tough conditions but enjoy considerable glamour.)

How the lions came to be in the Umfolozi is one of those curious little tales that this continent so often throws up. There were no lions left alive for many miles around when the park was first established in 1897. Then, in 1958, a solitary male began to make his way down from what was then Portuguese East Africa – a long journey on which he was soon dogged by hordes of men with guns, each of them anxious to demonstrate his masculinity by proving that a bullet can kill an animal.

Travelling at night and hiding by day, in the manner of lions, he continued to move south. The radio and newspapers gave daily reports on his latest movements and the steadily-growing band of killers trying to hunt him down homed in a bit closer each time he himself killed something to eat.

The game rangers, with a different interest, were also studying his progress with growing excitement as his direction pointed towards the safety of the Umfolozi Park, 'holding thumbs' as the South Africans say, that he would make it despite all the odds. There was considerable rejoicing among them when he finally crossed their boundary into the animal sanctuary, where no armed hunter dare set foot.

But of course the brave and determined male was there all by himself, and although the rangers could make sure that their fences were heightened and strengthened to keep him safely inside – and the neighbouring Zulu cattle safely outside – it seemed that he would indeed be the last wild lion in Zululand. Then, suddenly and mysteriously, several females joined him one dark night. On the official plans it was never supposed to be a lion park, because they bring additional hazards and work for all concerned, but nevertheless, there the females were and quite soon they began to breed and today there is a healthy lion population in Umfolozi, living in a natural balance with the other animals around them. How those mysterious females came to be there remains a mystery, and if you ask anybody who might be able to throw light on it the chances are that you will receive only an inscrutable gaze, and possibly a wink.

Enthusiasm for the Umfolozi must not cause one to overlook the equally impressive Hluhluwe Game Reserve (you will be albe to pronounce it if you know how to say Llandudno correctly, but Shlooshlooeey will do). It has also been a game reserve since 1897, which makes it a year older than the Kruger Park, and it can offer both black and white rhino, some lions and crocodiles, a huge variety of birds, and baboons, monkeys, hyenas, buffalo, nyala, kudu, wildebeest, zebra, giraffe, impala, waterbuck, warthogs and bushpigs, duikers, bushbuck, reedbuck and steenbuck and even leopards and cheetahs. Like the Umfolozi, the terrain ranges from the valleys to the heights, including the deep valley of the Hluhluwe River.

On the coast of Zululand the most spectacular part is no doubt that of St Lucia, with its vast estuary as much a living part of the sea as it is of the river system which feeds it from the land – which is why it offers to skin-divers the hazards of sharks, crocodiles, hippopotami and swordfish all in the same place. It also offers beaches, forests and mangrove swamps, with all the variety of plant and animal life which this suggests. The crocodiles are plentiful and it is doubtful if anyone needs to be told to be careful of them. They can be rather crafty too; I met a fisherman who was peacefully fishing by the edge of one of the St Lucia lakes one day when he heard a very slight rustle behind him. Fortunately for him, he looked round because it was a very large crocodile. It must have come out of the water some distance away and was very quietly stalking him, approaching through the bushes with the clear intention of rushing him in the next few seconds and taking him straight on into the water. Within the next few seconds the fisherman was quite a long distance away.

The lake is divided by islands into two main sections, and one section is about 16 miles long and the other some 25, while most of it is very shallow, being only about five feet deep, which of course increases the warmth of the water and the quantity of life in it. In the area around it there are various species of buck to be seen.

The Mkuze Game Reserve is another of those which tends to be comparatively under-appreciated, being a piece of protected wilderness of great natural beauty, distinguished by its parkland and particularly well-equipped for the keen photographer with its many artfully-placed hides.

Sordwana Bay is approached through Tsongaland, one of the most underdeveloped areas of tribal land in South Africa. Once you have descended the pass over the Ubombo mountains you will travel for miles through dense bush and lightly-forested country where there appear to be virtually no trading stores, schools, mission stations, farms, hospitals or anything except rather desolate little settlements of huts in the bush, where the people will offer wooden carvings by the roadside for very modest prices. Their wooden platters last much longer than factory-made glazed ones and are more interesting, since each one is carefully carved by hand; do not bargain with them too hard about the price – they need the money more than you do.

From here on to the border of Mocambique, where the Kosi Bay reserve lies, the authorities seem to be getting increasingly sensitive about people moving about, anxious to prevent unauthorized visitors, anxious about contact between Blacks and Whites and generally in a tense and rather aggressive state. Presumably this is because of the proximity of the former Portuguese, now independent, territory which might offer crossing-points for anti-government activists. Missionaries working in the area are much watched over and often interfered with by Pretoria, and actively discouraged if they happen to be Catholic. Altogether, whatever the reasons for the official mood of anxiety about the area, you are advised to apply long in advance for the necessary permits and permissions and bookings if you intend to visit Kosi Bay or you will come up against the forbidding face of South African officialdom.

Sordwana Bay, though it lies in the same region, does not seem to excite the authorities so much and one may go there without bookings or permits. It is a fine stretch of coastline approached by a road which gets progressively more sandy and a four-wheel drive vehicle or a truck is recommended.

The approach through the sandy dunes and lala palms is one of the best aspects of Sordwana Bay – which itself is much too popular for comfort and truck loads of frequently unpleasantly boisterous and noisy people crowd the limited camping sites to capacity on every public holiday. Many of them come all the way from the Free State, often bringing their black servants with them in the back of their trucks to minister to them while they disport themselves. But the men who run the reserve are a pleasant and helpful group.

One goes to game reserves to meet animals, rather than people, so it is perhaps of no great importance that for the past few years Pretoria has been making its heavy hand felt in some of these parts, such as Kosi Bay and the surrounding Tsongaland country. However, for those who do like to mix freely with the people of any area which they are visiting, and who do not enjoy being told by some grim little official that they are forbidden to fraternise with the local inhabitants, one should note that Zululand is in the process of becoming independent as the country of Kwazulu and that without doubt, as soon as this happens, the emissaries of Pretoria will go back where they belong, taking their racial rules and regulations with them. Then people visiting the game parks of Zululand, or Kwazulu, will presumably be able to mingle with other people there in the normal way. Let us hope that the government of Kwazulu will also be as efficient at running game parks as their predecessors have been.

And speaking of Pretoria – one of the best wildlife reserves in the Transvaal lies just a few miles outside the capital, but not only is it hardly known to the public but it is scarcely open to them either. This is the Rietvlei game reserve, about eight miles south of Pretoria. It is a piece of the Transvaal maintained very much as it was 100 years ago, with a good quantity of indigenous wildlife running almost free, only a few hundred yards from one of the main highways between Pretoria and the towns of the western reef. The public are to a large measure kept out of it for the benefit of scientists who want to study it. The South African public are still in an early stage of learning how not to pollute their environment and unfortunately have the habit of flinging broken bottles, empty cans, cigarette packets and any other debris around them when they go out into the veld for a picnic. Since this particular little park does not have the budget to provide the necessary African workers to clean up the mess and the necessary white officials to prevent the visitors doing even more harm, for the time being they simply keep the visitors out.

However, as the people gradually learn that the veld is neither infinitely large nor entirely self-cleansing, and as the Province develops a bigger budget for this type of amenity, no doubt this valuable and interesting little park will also become available to the general visitor. Certainly, those members of the public who have been allowed in, such as the yachtsmen who sail on the dam, have created no noticeable extra wear and tear on the environment and their little sailing craft are very picturesque as they glide to and fro against the backdrop of reeds and lakeside trees.

One of the nicest game parks in the Transvaal is the one at Loskop Dam, much closer to the main centres than the Kruger Park (about 110 miles from Johannesburg) and situated among the hills and valleys all around the great dam itself. The dam was built during the depression of the thirties, combining the creation of work for the jobless in that tough period, with the construction of a major dam on the Olifants River, which has worked out exceedingly well both as a source of irrigation water for the farms below and as an important conservation and amenity area in its own right.

The park itself is conceived very much as a recreational area, with ample space for caravans and tents in an attractive site right by the edge of the dam. There are furnished bungalows available – book in advance – a pleasant restaurant, shopping facilities and lots of places for children to play on the camping side of the dam. Then on the other side there is the game reserve, which has a good variety of wildlife species including a large number of the mighty eland, tame enough to approach within less than 100 yards, and quite a few rhino. The game rangers sometimes patrol on horseback and having once been chased by a charging rhino while on horseback one can sympathise with their respect for their irrascible friends of the nose-horn.

There are quite a few private game reserves in the Transvaal. Some of them started out as private shooting areas and developed into breeding ranches and there is now a well-established trade in indigenous animals; if you see a giraffe being carefully conveyed in a specially made truck, it is probably in transit between two such ranches.

One of the biggest of them is the Sabie-Sand Game Reserve adjoining the Kruger Park, which was formed by the amalgamation of a number of large farms totalling more than 150,000 acres. Its wildlife population includes roughly 25,000 impala, 3,000 wildebeest, 2,000 zebra, 1,000 giraffe and 500 kudu, as well as some waterbuck and the full range of predators – lions, jackals, hyenas, leopards, cheetahs and wild dogs. If you are well-connected you might meet someone who owns a share in one of the farms comprising this or one of the smaller private reserves in the area, and be invited for a weekend of Africa in the wild, in luxury.

If not, however, you can pay your own way and be admitted to part of the Sabie-Sand Game Reserve at the farm known as Malamala, which has a well-appointed camp for paying guests and provides good food as well as guides, transport and the very best of viewing facilities at an all-in price. It is not cheap, but it is worth it.

11 Natal

Most people in Natal are Zulus. Of the whole tribe of 4,000,000 most of them live in Natal, with about 800,000 Whites, 500,000 Asians and some 40,000 Coloured people who are, of course, a mixture of all the main groups. The central part of what is now Natal was once the kingdom of Zululand (from about 1820 to 1880) and the working out of the country's policy of separate development could conceivably place it once more under Zulu control in this century. The Zulus certainly anticipate this, as their spokesman have made clear on numerous occasions.

The present kingdom of Zululand, known as the Homeland of Kwazulu, is fragmented into some 29 separate divisions of Natal, and the official plan is to unify this as far as possible by buying out white farmers and others in corridors between the segments of Zululand. The Zulu leader, Chief Gatsha Buthezeli, has made it plain that his people will only accept a much larger, unified territory if separate development is to remain the pattern – they intend Durban to be part of it. In the century and a half that they have lived together, the Whites and Zulus have learned to favour negotiation rather than warfare, so the future prospects for Natal are not necessarily alarming, though they should certainly be exciting.

The Zulus have a very special place in the South African national mystique and imagination because of their spectacular military record in the early days of their kingdom, their impressive warrior qualities of courage, discipline and determination, their pride of race which remains so great that when they go elsewhere in the country to work they demand segregation from members of other tribes. In Johannesburg they are very visible because they generally work as nightwatchmen in the buildings, wear huge ear-discs through distended ear lobes and carry knobkerries. (When they pursue anybody they see trying to break into one of 'their' buildings they rush out into the street with a bloodcurdling bellow of 'bulala! bulala!' (kill, kill) other Zulu watchmen instantly take up the cry and the culprit is lucky if he falls into the hands of the comparatively merciful South African Police before the Zulus get him). On the mines they work as Police 'boys', and since they are amongst the tallest people in South Africa their presence in uniform, armed with a sjambok or assegai, is impressive. They do not work underground in the mines, leaving that to other tribes and explaining if asked; 'I will go under the ground when I am dead, but that is not yet.'

White people who have to deal with them generally treat them with a rather special respect. They are a friendly people and by no means arrogant, but their pride is considerable and it is ill-advised to try a hectoring or even patronising approach with them.

The authorities know them particularly as a people who are capable of disciplined, concerted action to a greater extent than any other group of black people in the country. Over the years they have demonstrated this time and again, most impressively in their military actions when they threw their impis into battle in formidable orderly ranks and formations, but also in smaller actions over the years, when they have felt that their grievances were being overlooked. This reflects, as well as tribal solidarity, an attitude of very long standing that if chiefs or their equivalents were not governing satisfactorily then they must be called to account. The despotism of figures like Shaku and Dingaan was unusual – a more democratic system was the normal custom not only among the Zulus but among the other tribes as well, and this attitude of mind persists.

The Zulus owe their fame to the military genius of Shaka, but he built on what had already been established by Dingiswayo, who was not a Zulu but a Mthethwa.

17 Eastern Cape. The Katberg Pass
18 Looking into the Oribi Gorge, Natal

One has to bear in mind that the Zulus are only part of the great Nguni group, although the four million Zulus are the biggest and most prominent tribe among those speaking Nguni languages. The Xhosas number just under four million and are ahead of the Zulus in achieving independence for their Transkei homeland, and there are others like the Bhaca and Tsonga, who have also had their great chiefs, warriors, poets and wise men.

But it was Dingiswayo, who became chief of the Mthethwa round about 1790 and made the great innovation of combining education with military training which was to be the first stepping-stone to the new kingdom. There is a well-established myth in South Africa that Dingiswayo learned his new ideas from contact with white men. In 1875 Theophilus Shepstone, Governor of Natal, expressed it in a paper as follows:

> It seems that in his travels Dingiswayo had reached the Cape Colony, and must have lived with or entered the service of some colonist . . . It was during his stay in the Cape Colony that he acquired the information, or made the observations, which were to effect the great change in his native land and the surrounding countries . . . He learned the strength of standing armies, the value of discipline and training, as compared with the mobs called armies in his own country. He saw that if he could gain possession of his tribe he could gratify his ambition. He had heard of or seen bodies of civilized soldiers. He had ascertained that they were divided into regiments and companies, with regularly appointed officers, and he thought that all soldiers were bachelors. He had no sooner got possession of power than he set to work to organise his tribe in accordance with these ideas.

However, there is no evidence to support this tale and later authorities have reduced it to the level of 'no more than wild speculation.' It fits, to some extent, subsequent events and it also fits white attitudes, particularly current in the nineteenth century and surviving in some quarters well into the twentieth, that black people can achieve nothing of

19 An African Mine-Dancer

consequence unless they first learn how to do it from white people. One thinks of the historians who constructed theories about mysterious white visitors coming into the interior many centuries ago to build Zimbabwe, and their rage at the suggestion that the Africans might have built it themselves.

In any case, wherever he got the idea from, Dingiswayo blended the educational and military systems of his people and put all the young men into regiments in what amounted to a standing army. They had their own distinctive shields and dress and were formed of young men from the same age groups, and this gave an immediate advantage over the neighbouring tribes who only organised ad hoc fighting parties when the occasion arose. In addition, he set about imposing a sort of Pax Dingiswayo in his area, and a peacemaker with an army behind him often comes to control a country.

Shaka, an illegitimate child with a romantic family background raised in the neighbouring Zulu tribe, was conscripted into Dingiswayo's army and rapidly made his way up through outstanding military talent. There are heroic legends about him among both white and black South Africans, and he seems to have been brave and wily as well as clear-thinking. There is a story which relates how he went out alone one night to hunt down a hyena which had seized a girl and was dragging her away; the hyena is an animal which excites a peculiar dread amongst most African tribesmen, with a collection of eerie tales to match stories of werewolves in Eastern Europe.

The chief of the Zulus, Senzangakona, died in about 1816. His son, who was meant to succeed him, was assassinated. Shaka moved in, already influential enough in the Mthethwa army to take over the Zulu chieftainship with their backing.

Immediately, he applied the Mthethwa system to the Zulus, built up an army of bachelor soliders not allowed to marry until they were 40, and armed them with a short stabbing spear instead of the traditional longer throwing spear. He developed his own military tactics, including a variant of the classical Grecian 'dilemma' formation: a regiment of double strength attacking in the centre with two long horns of men reaching out to either side ready to close in and encircle the enemy for the final onslaught at the ominous chant of 'ingenile pagati' ('it has entered inside' – meaning, the enemy is surrounded), roared out and transmitted in seconds from man to man from one end of the battlefield to the other.

Very soon Shaka was building up his kingdom by conquering all around him, although he did not embrace the Mthethwas until after Dingiswayo had died. By the early 1820's he had an army of some 50,000 men and a women's regiment of 10,000 – and ruled over most of what is now Natal. He was ruthless, swallowing up the conquered with all their possessions into his own confederacy, killing off ruling houses including their women and children, always accompanied by his executioners to deal with anybody suspected of treachery.

So rapid was the increase of his military kingdom and so great the wave effect of other great chiefs and their people fleeing before it, that the repercussions were felt from the Cape to the shores of Lake Tanganyika – throughout a fifth of the whole gigantic continent of Africa.

While this was going on, the first white settlers were also arriving on the scene. The English-speaking contingent were the first to arrive in the form of a handful of traders who came by sea from Cape Town in 1824 and settled themselves around Port Natal, the forerunner of Durban. The Afrikaners were also on their way overland, but they arrived somewhat later, during the reign of Shaka's successor, his half-brother Dingaan.

Shaka, in his later years, became increasingly blood-thirsty and tyrannical and in 1828 brother Dingaan, helped by some friends, assassinated him and took over.

The white traders and missionaries gradually extended their influence in the kingdom, and although Dingaan referred to them as 'his' white men, by 1830 he was getting reports that white men were plotting to steal his kingdom. By 1834 merchants and others from Cape Town in fact petitioned the British Government to annex Port Natal and the surrounding area, but the British Government could see no profit in it.

Dingaan's real troubles began, however, when the first Boer Voortrekkers appeared over the Drakensberg mountains in 1837. They brought their ox-wagons with them, carrying them in pieces over the rugged mountains, with their guns and Bibles, and their herds. They were looking for land.

The white traders already precariously established there were glad to see these potential allies arriving. The Boer leader, Piet Retief, went to establish friendly relations with Dingaan and to try and negotiate some sort of treaty for the use of land in his kingdom. What followed was to have fatal results, both for Piet Retief and the Zulu kingdom.

After the usual courtesies, exchanges of presents, displays of warriors and cattle and so forth, they got down to business and Piet Retief explained through a trader interpreter what he wanted. Dingaan said eventually that he was, 'almost inclined' to let the Boers have the land they asked for, but first he wanted a demonstration of their loyalty and goodwill to him. He wanted Piet Retief and his fellow-Boers to go and recover for him a large quantity of cattle which had been stolen by chief Sekonyela's people. This Retief promised to do.

He went back and reported that things were going favourably, and immediately Boers began streaming over the Drakensberg and spreading out with their wagons and animals in upper Natal, without waiting for the next stage of the formalities. Retief, meanwhile, went off to Sekonyela's territory to fulfil his part of the bargain. He tricked Sekonyela into a meeting in a missionary's garden, handcuffed him and told him he would not be released until the stolen cattle, together with quantities of horses and guns were provided. These were duly produced.

At this point, striving no doubt to make the best of his bargain, Retief began to overplay his hand. Instead of simply handing over the cattle, horses and guns which he had seized on Dingaan's behalf, he sent him a message lecturing him about what happened to 'bad kings' and apparently trying to soften Dingaan up, as it were, so as to get the best possible treaty agreement. It had quite the reverse effect. Dingaan was already in serious doubt about the wisdom of allowing any further white men to settle in his kingdom and influential councillors were constantly telling him that this was the thin end of the wedge, that once the white men had a foothold in an African kingdom they soon would come to rule it. Dingaan decided that Piet Retief was not to be trusted and must be killed.

Retief arrived at the royal kraal of Mgungundlovu in February 1838 with the captured cattle and an entourage of 100. Dingaan entertained them in the royal manner and after a few days he put his mark on the coveted treaty, giving Retief and his people the use of the land 'from the place called Port Natal . . . and from the Tugela to the Umzimvubu, and from the sea to the North . . .' Then the festivities went on, and the noose began to close.

Retief and his party were invited to watch a war dance performed by two regiments. In such dances to this day there is always a rather frightening moment when the warriors rush up at the guests as if to fall upon them, but stop a few feet short and instead give the royal salute of 'Bayete.' This time they did not stop. They swept right round the 70 Voortrekkers and their 30 Coloured attendants, surrounded them, seized them and bound them firmly. Then they dragged them away to the execution hill and clubbed some of them to death and impaled others.

From there they swept on to attack the Boers in their encampments, killing about 40 men, 56 women and 185 children and more than 200 Coloured servants at the place which came to be known as Weenen (Mourning or Weeping). They attacked one white group after another and in Port Natal itself they burnt the buildings to the ground and the Whites had to flee from the land and take refuge on a ship which happened to be lying at harbour. They had carried out the threat which the black man has reiterated down the centuries – that they would drive the white man into the sea.

But the victory was not to last. After some further setbacks, the Boers brought in an experienced commando leader, Andries Pretorius, who organized a disciplined commando of 500 men supported by 57 wagons and taking with them a cannon as well as their rifles they rode into Zululand to take on the Zulu army. When their scouts reported the Zulus approaching in force, the Boers drew up their wagons into their defensive laager formation on the bank of the Ncome river, in a position of their own choosing. They prayed for victory, and vowed to build a church to commemorate the occasion if victory was granted them. Then the Zulus attacked with a force of about 10,000 men. The Boers mowed them down systematically as wave after wave of them tried to charge and cross the river until eventually, it is said, the river ran red with blood. This was the Boer's revenge, the Battle of Blood River, and it plays a large part in the nation's memory, being celebrated now as a public holiday, the Day of the Covenant.

After the battle the Boers pushed on right to the royal kraal itself, Dingaan fleeing before them. There, on the execution hill, they found their treaty to the land of Natal in a leather bag among the corpses. For Dingaan this was the beginning of the end. His half-brother Mpande joined forces with the Boers against him and together they finally routed his armies, the Boers taking about 36,000 of his cattle after the final battle. They proclaimed Mpande king of the Zulus, but vassal of the Natal Republic which they set up.

Mpande's reign was peaceful and by the time he died in 1872, the Zulu nation had once again built up its herds of cattle and its regiments of warriors. They were to fight one more great battle – this time against the British army, at Isandhlwana. The force which tried to crush them finally consisted of 7000 British troops, about the same number of African levies and 1000 volunteers, under Lord Chelmsford. The noble lord elected to ignore the advice of President Paul Kruger that the Zulus were to be treated with great caution, that careful scouting was essential and that the army should at all times entrench its camps. The result was the worst military disaster that Britain had suffered since the Crimean War. The Zulu army attacked the central column of troops so fast that they caught them unprepared and although they still relied on stabbing spears against rifles they slaughtered 1600 soldiers.

Fifty years later Hugh Tracy, the authority on African music, found a very old Zulu induna who had been a young warrior at the Battle of Isandhlwana and asked him if he still remembered the battle. 'Oh yes,' said the old man, nodding and chuckling, 'we let out their tea on that day.'

The army recovered from the reverse and finally defeated the Zulus at Ulundi later the same year, after which their kingdom was split up into 13 separate territories each under a chief – the 'divide and rule' tactic.

The British had arrived on the scene largely because of pressure from the London Missionary Society, claiming that the Boers were exterminating the Zulus. They brought the Boer Republic of Natal to an end after only five years of existence as a separate state, occupying it in 1842. Apart from a humanitarian concern about the survival of the Zulus they were also worried that the Voortrekker methods would cause serious instability along Natal's frontier with their Cape Colony.

Although the Republic as such did not survive long, it had set the pattern for white occupation of the area. The Boers had to deal with the question of citizenship and they laid down guidelines which expressed the essence of Apartheid and the separate racial development which was still the official Afrikaner government philosophy more than a century later.

The Voortrekkers assumed their black servants, on whom they were dependent, to be a different sub-species and their language has a special term for them – 'skepsels' (creatures) as opposed to 'mense' (people). There was no question, therefore, of these creatures being admitted to citizenship. Other white people could be accepted into the community once their loyalty was well established, but non-whites were only allowed to be in the Republic in the capacity of servants. They were not permitted to own any land, or firearms, or horses, to take any part in political processes, and indeed they were not allowed to move about at all unless they carried a pass signed by a white employer.

The Voortrekkers believed, and many of their descendants will still argue, that these principles of social order were laid down in the Bible, as they interpreted it. The Oxford History says: 'so engrained were they in the Voortrekker mind that they were unhesitatingly translated into law in the first Voortrekker Republic. That was what custom prescribed, self-interest demanded and God ordained. That was how it had always been and always must be in South Africa.'

But the Blacks do not share this view of their destiny and the Zulus of Natal and Zululand remain today a people still capable of much concerted, disciplined action, with qualities of stoicism, courage and pride which remain an important factor in the country's life. Zulu rickshaw boys, while fine, jovial characters with a prominent place in tourist activities on the beachfront at Durban, should not be taken as too symbolic a figure for the current role and future prospects of the nation, any more than a seaside entertainer at Blackpool should be taken for John Bull.

The Indians in Natal were very late arrivals on the scene but they have also made a very interesting and visible contribution to the cultural and economic life of the province. The white-washed Hindu temples among the deep green cane-fields on the old road north, with the blue sea behind them glittering in the sun, offer an exotic glimpse of the life of another continent, with its own gods, its music, different faces, clothes, customs and foods.

Brought out originally as plantation labourers in the 1860's, the Indians have taken well to Natal and though many of them are still working humbly among the sugar canes, many others have built up big businesses – the Indian market-places, streets and blocks of Indian shops are among Durban's greatest attractions. Many of the Indians have done very well financially too, with their talent for living on the job, involving their whole family in it and working hours that no European in this century would consider possible.

The attitude of other groups to them is ambivalent, and they have had their hard times, including two general massacres this century when the Zulus attacked them throughout Natal. White South Africans admire their curries in particular and are interested and entertained by the more colourful of their religious ceremonies and festivals – even fire-walking is to be seen near Durban.

They are impressed by the way an Indian will start off with virtually no capital, live with his whole family in one or two tiny rooms on top of or behind his little shop, and work seven days a week, year in and year out, selling half-pounds of sugar and pinches of salt and an occasional yard of cloth, slowly building up his little business and eventually managing to send a son or daughter to university. But if the same Indian accumulates enough money to buy a flashy motor-car the white and black South African is often annoyed and envious.

For years there was a policy of repatriating Indians by offering them not only a free passage to India but a going away present of ten pounds as well. Few took it, preferring to stay in the country where they were born. The Group Areas Act has been invoked against them, pushing them out of shops and houses where they have been established near the city centre of Durban for generations. In recent years official attitudes towards them seem to have become much more sympathetic and although they have been excluded from the white universities and now have a 'separate but equal' racially segregated university in Natal, it is generally said to be well-equipped and in most ways of a high standard, and the townships which have been set aside for Indian occupation are mostly well laid out and serviced, with some very high quality housing among them.

The Zulu attacks on them – rather half-heartedly restrained by the South African white armed forces – seem to have been fomented by racial jealousy of them as interlopers who appeared to be gradually gaining a better share of Natal and of life in general than the Zulus themselves. With no commercial culture, few instrumental skills applicable to modern technology and not much horticultural ability either, the Zulus over the past century have not been able to compete with the Indians very successfully in the push towards material well-being, so they turned in the end to their ancient prowess as warriors to try and redress the balance.

Apart from the picturesque tribal surroundings where

Zulus live in their traditional beehive-shaped huts on the green hills overlooking the rivers, most of them live in township housing on the outskirts of Durban and the other urban centres, and although some of this housing is well-established and quite pleasant, there have also been some notorious slums.

One of the worst of these was Cato Manor, where the 'beerhall riots' erupted in 1959. The riots were the culmination of many grievances and deprivations of people living in a squalid semi-urban slum, but they got their name from the fact that among the organizers of the first demonstrations were many 'shebeen queens'. These were big, determined Zulu women who made a living by brewing illegal beer to sell to the menfolk and for weddings and other feasts; they resented the competition of the legal, official beer-halls run by the City Council so much that they finally stormed into the city in a huge womens' impi armed with clubs, surged into the beerhalls, beat up and chased out the men who were drinking there and polluted the beer in the tanks in what one can only call a highly personal manner.

There is no need to recall all the incidents of that period here, but there were some tense and exceedingly dangerous moments in which the safety of the whole city trembled in the balance. One man, a police major called Jerry van der Merwe, played a most heroic role by turning back a horde of people armed with clubs, knives, spears, axes and other weapons, who were coming down the main road into Durban, heading for the jail to release some of their leaders. They were met by Jerry van der Merwe at the head of a column of armoured cars and other police vehicles, and as the African crowd came down the road and the armoured cars with their machine guns came up it the situation looked more and more terrifying.

The major halted his vehicles, ordered their gun-turrets turned the other way, walked out ahead of them entirely by himself, a huge man with his revolver jammed informally into the front of his belt, held up his hand and began talking to the crowd in Zulu as they came up to him. They came to a stop. He explained to them that if they tried to go any further his men would open fire on them and then he said: 'although I am only a policeman, I know you have some grievances, and if you get your spokesmen to tell me what they are, I will go and tell the government what you have said, this will be better than fighting.' Such was his personal authority that the huge mob finally accepted this arrangement and dispersed at the end of the day without bloodshed.

But there was another occasion at that period when nine young policemen – five Whites and four Blacks – decided to go on a beer raid into the heart of the slum on a Sunday, 'The Day of the Great Thirst' as a South African judge once called it. The mob turned on them and hacked them to death, surging in on them as they stood in a ring firing their revolvers into the crowd which kept coming forward chanting: 'their bullets will soon be finished.'

The shooting at Sharpeville followed not long after that, in which policemen opened fire on another crowd and killed 69 people, and although there was no direct link between the incidents, some people have seen it as a modern re-enactment of the traditional Boer response to an attack on any of their people – just another answer in the dangerous dialogue between the races in this violent continent.

Port Natal, once wiped out overnight by a quite small impi, is today Durban, one of the most important ports on the east coast of Africa. It is also a leading holiday centre where Transvalers in particular can get away, in a few hours drive on the motorway, from their own bleak highveld winters to the warm sub-tropical beaches. Alas, they have to tread rather warily along those beaches nowadays lest they step in an oil slick. The fleets of shipping bring penalties as well as rewards.

One of the most interesting amenities in Durban is the oceanarium, a great sea-water aquarium pierced with viewing windows and surrounded by walkways at different levels, so that one can literally walk up to within two or three feet of a six-foot tiger shark going about its affairs. It is well-stocked with representatives of practically all the marine species to be found in these waters and well run, in the South African manner.

The coast south of Durban is also a much sought after holiday and retirement area, and the golden beaches with their backing of dense green scrub and low jungle are certainly attractive. Again, there are some reservations about this 'holiday paradise'. It is very full of buildings and people – so much so that there is hardly a camping site to be found near the beach within 50 miles of Durban, because all the space has been taken up by hotels and blocks of flats. If one remembers it as it was not many years ago, with a few bungalows and smallish boarding-houses and hotels scattered along the coastline, well surrounded by palms and dense bush, no spot of dirt on the beaches, plenty of places where people without much money could put up a tent under the trees and have an open-air holiday next to the sea, then of course the transition to brash, commercially-exploited Holidayland is rather jarring, but no doubt it compares well with various even more crowded coastal resorts elsewhere in the world.

North of Durban, though, the coast is not nearly so built up and there is a splendid highway going north to the fine Natal game parks. Inland, towards the Drakensberg there is peaceful Pietermaritzburg, which must be one of the nicest places in the world to retire. A couple of thousand feet above sea level, it still has a pleasantly warm climate practically all year round, but never gets as muggily humid as Durban does during the summer. From Pietermaritzburg on, one is out of the sub-tropical coastal plains with their sugar-cane fields and dense undergrowth interspersed with palm-trees, and into the 'Natal Midlands' of fine wide farms with some of the best grassland in the country.

12 The Homelands

The development of the Bantu Homelands is highly controversial. Much development and progress has been achieved under this policy, but at the same time many lives have been thwarted and stunted by it. This is very much a case where there are two sides to the story, and we shall try to look at both of them. One must try to be fair and objective and it is not the writer's function, in this context, to try and propagandize for or against a particular policy, but it is also only fair to state at the outset that my own prejudice is against the whole concept of racial separation.

First, the good news. The development of the eight homelands, at its best, has been described as 'an exercise in decolonisation' and this is a very helpful formulation of the policy. The great desire is for orderly transition – everything must go smoothly, the new 'country' itself must be built up to become as economically viable as possible, its services effectively organised, native personnel trained to take over from the previous colonial, or in this case white South African, administrators. Powers, responsibilities and budgets must be carefully transferred in a series of graded steps, from limited self-government to the ultimate launch into full independence with all its promises and risks.

The processes applied in the Transkei, for example, the first of the homelands to be prepared fully for independence, show striking parallels with the way the British handed over in Kenya – a classic exercise in successful decolonisation. South Africa still had an embassy in Kenya at the time and there can be no doubt that Pretoria was most impressed at how well it all went, and how creditably it all worked out for the British when they finally hauled down the Union Jack, shook hands and marched out of office. Many British remained to continue living and working happily in a peaceful Kenya for years.

That was the good example. The bad one was what happened in the former Belgian Congo, when the Belgians literally switched off the lights and water and ran for it, leaving the country totally unprepared for running itself, with only a handful of graduates and virtually no number two men ready to step into the vacant shoes of their predecessors. Rioting, chaos, cannibalism, atrocities, famine and every type of human disaster and social breakdown followed and it took the Congo years of agony to begin to pull itself together again. The South Africans are determined that this will not happen in their country and much of their over-reaction to minor disturbances, or even criticism, probably relates to anxiety on this score.

The theory itself on which the separate development of the homeland rests is nothing new in South African history, as we have already seen. The fundamental question of 'Who Is A Citizen?' had been asked and answered long since, and formally enshrined in the constitution of the short-lived Boer republic in Natal, among others. Blacks, who were a different order of being, could never become citizens in white South Africa – but they could be citizens in their own country, or countries. Ideally, they should be the best of neighbours, living on terms of great friendliness and harmony with white South Africa, and if they wished to visit it to work then of course they could do so, under strictly controlled conditions as foreign workers temporarily in the country. Logically too, therefore, white South Africans should also enter or work in the homelands with the permission of the inhabitants, and in fact for many years now white officials concerned with administering the homelands have imposed many restrictions on other non-resident whites moving through the territories. This they do with a certain pride, pointing out when criticised that 'they have got to have special passes and permits to be in our areas, so we have also got to have special permits to be in their areas. It's only fair.'

Dr Hendrik Verwoerd, who was Prime Minister until his assassination in 1966, brought the theory up to date and emphasized its positive aspects, developing the idea of separate freedoms, which was enthusiastically taken up by the ruling National Party, and this positive and enthusiastic approach to the whole programme remains very striking and, whatever its origins, not entirely unattractive.

Dr Verwoerd believed, he told Parliament, that the development of South Africa on this basis 'will create so much friendship, so much gratitude, so many mutual interests in the process of the propulsive development that there will no longer be hostile Bantu states, but that there will arise what I call a Commonwealth, founded on common interests and linked together by common interests.'

This tied in perfectly with the Afrikaners' sense of national destiny, and also provided a much more attractive rationale for racial separatism than talk of keeping the black man in his place to provide cheap labour for the Whites. The Johannesburg newspaper, *The Star,* said of Verwoerd: 'His theory of separate freedoms was his most important contribution to Afrikaner Nationalism, oppressed as it was with an uneasy sense of guilt before the accusing eyes of the world. It was able to hold up its head again.'

A recent government monograph *(A State in the Making)* puts it this way:

> In South Africa, as in Europe, a number of diverse peoples live side by side, each proud of the characters which make them what they are, each anxious to retain them, while on the other hand, modern conditions demand a growing degree of economic co-operation between them in the interests of improved living standards and economic stability. Therefore, in Africa as in Europe, the aim must be to bring about economic co-operation between peoples without destroying the basic characters of the individual groups. In short, what is being attempted, whether it be in Europe or in South Africa, is one and the same thing, political independence coupled with economic interdependence. South Africa's policy, so often stated, is to lead

the less developed black nations within her borders to complete political independence; but it must be a stable independence and so she has put her resources in men, in materials, in money and ideas at their disposal, that they shall be given every possible chance of achieving stability, prosperity and a worthy place in the modern world. This applies to all the Bantu peoples of South Africa: all are being led to independent nationhood.

One must note the strong sense of the white man's mission, a motif which recurs again and again, carrying with it the proviso that 'we know what is best for you.' It is expressed, for example, in the preamble to the 1966 Prevention of Improper Interference Bill, which seeks to prevent Whites taking any part in black politics. It says, inter alia: ' . . . the whites as the guardians of the other population groups accept their mission to lead the non-white population groups to self-realisation and to safeguard them against political exploitation by others as the sole guarantee for the continued existence of both their own and the other population groups . . . .'

One must bear this attitude in mind when confronted with the occasional furious outbursts of homeland leaders to the general effect that they never wanted this separate racial development in the first place – but we shall return to this aspect.

There are eight main groups due to get their own homelands. The first is the Xhosa, with the Transkei. (The initial Xh is pronounced in the same way you would make a loud click to encourage a horse, by drawing the tip of your tongue explosively away from your palate, and then go straight on with the rest of the word. But if you cannot manage that, Kosa will do well enough, pronouced Kausa, with the accent on the first syllable.) The other groups are at various stages in the development of their territories towards independence, being the Zulus, Shangaans, Swazis, Southern Sothos, Northern Sothos and Vendas.

At the time of writing the homelands, or Bantustans as they have become popularly known, are said to consist of 113 fragments of land, although some authorities have said they

20 Eastern Buttress Amphitheatre viewed from Tendele Camp, Royal Natal National Park, Drakensberg

21 A West Cape vineyard

are split into as many as 296. The government is trying to consolidate these as far as is practicable, but cannot foresee reducing them to fewer fragments than 36 for the eight homelands. The biggest tribes will be the most split up: Kwazulu (four million people) will be split into ten pieces; there will be five fragments in two separate states (Transkei and Ciskei) for the 3.9 million Xhosas and six pieces for the 1.7 million Tswanas.

In addition to these, the programme is being actively applied in Namibia or South West Africa, although South Africa's possession of this territory is, to say the least, highly contentious. The tribes there have been allocated their respective homelands, with populations so far ranging from 211,000 for Ovamboland to a rather touching 'nil' for Bushmanland.

The Transkei, the first of these homelands to go into independence, is perhaps the showpiece and therefore one must not take it as completely typical of the others, but it is an official model for their development. Its territory forms a nice neat unit about the size of Denmark, some 16,500 square miles, including about 150 miles of some of the country's finest coastal land – the wild coast. This is a very different case to that of Kwazulu, say, still fragmented into 29 different pieces.

It is hilly country, of considerable natural grandeur. Great rivers cut through it and there are some notable peaks and valleys. The climate is generally mild, offering an interesting range both for people and other forms of life – sub-tropical on the coast, with snow not infrequent at higher points in winter.

The total population of the Transkei is about 3,570,000 which would give it an average population density of more than 200 per square mile. However, this would be a false figure since not only do many of its people spend most of their working lives outside the territory as migratory workers, but there are a great many other people who are designated as Transkei citizens although they have never seen the place, having been born somewhere else in South Africa. All the black people of the country have been allocated specific homelands according to their tribal origins, though many of

22 A view of Table Mountain fron Blouberg
23 Looking eastwards along the coast at Strandfontein, Cape Peninsula

them have lived in the cities for generations. This means that the homelands have a *de facto* population of the people actually living there and a *de jure* population which includes those tribal members living elsewhere but designated as citizens of the homeland. (The word 'tribes' itself has gradually become less acceptable and officialdom prefers to speak of 'ethnic groups', since one ethnic language group may be sub-divided into many smaller tribes, but tribes is a more convenient and familiar general term in this context.)

Some authorities would say that the territory is disastrously overcrowded, having regard to the fact that it is an agricultural area with a very limited technology and rudimentary industry. The South African government has poured money and manpower into the problem of improving the level of agricultural productivity in the Transkei for years, and anybody who has passed through the countryside there during the past 30 years will certainly confirm that its appearance has changed greatly for the better since this campaign began. Overpopulation by cattle-herding semi-nomadic tribesmen is just about the quickest way of destroying the natural balance of any area and reducing it to a desert, but as far as is possible this process has been arrested and even reversed in the Transkei, with much being done to combat soil erosion (which has been occuring over most of the farming areas of South Africa at a terrifying rate for at least a century, the desert sometimes advancing from the west into the Transvaal and Free State by as much as half a mile a year.)

The official explanation for the agricultural problems of this potentially rich countryside tends to stress the disadvantages of tribal custom rather than the effects of overcrowding, presumably since it is easier to do something about teaching people to change their farming habits than to give them more land or to shrink their population.

The South African experts – and to give them their due they are no amateurs when it comes to farming matters – estimate that the potential supply of both grain and animal protein of the Transkei could far exceed the requirements of the approximately eight million people who are expected to be living there in 70 to 80 years' time.

They have tried to start the new state off on the right lines by launching one of the biggest, most concerted attacks on improving an agricultural area ever mounted in Africa. Apart from reflecting the fact that white South Africa is both wealthy and determined this programme of course does point out the advantages of holding a great deal of power; you cannot move into a densely populated landscape the size of Denmark and set about working on it and systematically changing it radically unless you have almost total power over the inhabitants of that area, since various objections are bound to be raised (particularly about cattle culling in a pastoral community). Is that a good or bad thing? One can think about it.

Whatever the political morality of the issue, they set to work allocating what the planning committees considered to be the most suitable areas for people to live in, excising unproductive arable land, planning controlled grazing, putting up fences and putting in watering points for both people and animals. By 1968, according to the official figures, this project had involved constructing 1,392 dams, sinking 524 boreholes, beaconing and preserving the vegetation of 17,330 waterways, building 2,208 miles of diversion banks, 804 dipping tanks and putting up enough fencing to reach almost round the world – 24,400 miles of it – and 128,600 miles of grass strip.

The forests of the Transkei were developed from 40,000 acres in 1951 to 216,000 acres in 1969. It is a remarkable and worthwhile achievement and whatever one may think of the political theory underlying it, the fact remains that a generation of white administrative and technical workers have spent virtually their whole working lives labouring at this project – though backed up, let it not be forgotten, by an army of black workers – and they have something of great value to show for it. The Transkei is scheduled to take off into independence in 1976.

The form of government bequeathed by the South Africans to their emerging homelands is a fusion of tribal government with parliamentary democracy, based on the system which

Britain in turn bequeathed to South Africa. This means that the Legislative Assembly of the Transkei has an opposition, since it consists partly of elected members. The leader of the opposition, Mr Knowledge Guzana, has frequently complained that the ratio of 64 chiefs to 45 elected members favours the Establishment far too much, and in addition he is opposed to the whole idea of the Transkei becoming a separate state, wants it to stay open to Whites as well as Blacks with multi-racialism as the way of life, though not racial integration. Although he is an outspoken opponent of official policy one should place on record that he has not been prevented from having his say – though others to his left have certainly been silenced.

The Chief Minister himself, Paramount Chief Kaizer Matanzima, has always accepted the idea of self-government leading to independence, taken government promises at face value and finally called for the independence that he was promised all along. He has displayed a sense of timing and political drama, announcing among other things that there would be no Apartheid or racial discrimination in any form in the new Transkei, and that Whites would be able to have full citizenship there as well as Blacks.

When he first started making noises about demanding independence there was a certain amount of disbelief, not to say alarm, among many white people in South Africa, English-speaking as well as Afrikaans. It would be fair to say that a great many Whites thought that the whole concept of giving independence to African states within South Africa's borders was, if not an outright bluff, at least one of those promises that gets delayed and delayed indefinitely and never fulfilled.

As one who was working in Pretoria at the time, with access to some authoritative government advisers, it was clear that whatever impression the white electorate may have had, the government had in fact long since made up its mind to go ahead with the adventure of granting independence when the time came. If there were to be any delay it would be used to develop the homelands more fully in the direction of being viable little countries rather than as a tactic of delaying the course of history. I also asked some of the ministers-to-be of the Lebowa homeland in the northern Transvaal, another one nearing independence, what exactly they understood by the term independence. One of them replied – there were several present at the occasion and they all signified agreement – 'we understand independence to mean full and total political independence, with full powers to run your own country, exactly the same as that which is enjoyed by the United Kingdom, for example, or France or the United States.'

I repeated this unequivocal answer to the Commissioner General of the territory, Mr Gert Bezuidenhout, a former National Party politician, asking the inevitable question about the potential dangers of enclave independent states pursuing policies totally at variance with those of their big neighbour. What would happen for example, if one of the independent homeland states decided to invite the Russian army to set up a base on its territory? He had thought about it and he was quite definite in his answer too: 'I took on this job with one single goal – to see the people of Lebowa achieve their full independence and nothing less, and there is no double-talk or doubt about it.' He hoped that they, and others in the same position, would not do anything that might seriously embarrass South Africa, 'but if they want to do anything like that, it's up to them.' By the same token, of course, South Africa would try not to do anything to put them in a difficult spot. A tough, energetic Afrikaner, crippled by fanatical rugby-playing in his youth and with the reputation of being honest to the bone, if Gert Bezuidenhout did not mean and believe every word that he said, then he certainly fooled me.

There is of course a considerable identity of interests between the little client states in the making and their large, rich and powerful patron and progenitor, South Africa. Chief Lucas Mangope, Chief Minister of the Bophuthatswana homeland, said on the occasion of his homeland achieving the status of self-governing territory, in 1972: ' . . . if South Africa falls, we fall. South Africa's foes are our foes. I have said it on many occasions before and I affirm it again today in the name of my people.'

But if one is trying to look into the future, one should perhaps contrast this type of comment with another reaction, about a year later, when President Idi Amin of Uganda was at a peak of violence, his country in near chaos and tens of thousands of people had been slaughtered there. A documentary film about him was brought to Johannesburg and a group of leading African businessmen and other community leaders were invited to join some white counterparts in viewing it. After the film, which gave a reasonably fair portrayal of Amin at the time, the Whites who had arranged the evening asked the Blacks how they would like to have Amin running South Africa. To their considerable shock and disappointment, the Africans answered to a man that although they fully understood the nature of the disasters which had followed Amin's particular form of one-man rule, they would rather have him in charge of South Africa than the present government. As one of them put it, bluntly: 'at least he is one of our own.'

As the various homelands move into independence, they will tend to have reasonably moderate leaders at the helm at the time of being granted independence. What will happen after that is a question more for prophets than political analysts.

In the foregoing, I have tried to portray the homelands project in optimistic terms, to try and give a fair impression of the positive side which South African officialdom always accuses overseas writers of ignoring. But there are other, less pleasant aspects.

To begin with, whatever language politicians might use to dress it up in these more sensitive times, the basic reason for the whole policy is quite simply that the governing Whites do not want the Blacks in 'their' country on any basis other than that of servants, with minimal human rights and no political rights at all. This has been stated again and again in various forms by Afrikaner National Party leaders and although in recent years they have tried to put it more tactfully, assisted by the Verwoerd doctrine of separate freedoms, nothing has changed in their basic motives for enforcing this policy.

Prime Minister John Vorster put it like this in 1968 in Parliament:

> 'The fact of the matter is this: we need them, because they work for us . . . but the fact that they work for us can never – if one accepts this as one's own criterion one will be signing one's own death sentence now – entitle them to claim political rights. Not now, nor in the future. It makes no difference whether they are here with any degree of permanency or not . . . under no circumstances can we grant them those political rights in our territory, neither now nor ever.

Nor is there any need to believe smooth assurances of 'consultation' with the Blacks and of their widespread enthusiasm for the project. Black leaders have stated their opposition to the programme at every stage, detailing their reasons and a massive apparatus of coercion has been set up both to force them into formal acceptance of the homelands separate development policy and then forcibly to 'resettle' hundreds of thousands of miserably unwilling black people in the areas allocated to them. I have seen the night sky over Pondoland lit up as far as the horizon by burning huts during riots provoked by the enforcement of homeland measures in the early 1960's, and seen the remains of people machine-gunned at close range during similar riots, for the same basic causes, in the Bafurutse Reserve in the Transvaal bushveld. One could almost say that the Blacks have been forced into their so-called homelands at the point of a gun, and when they have eventually accepted the situation they have made it abundantly clear that they do so in the spirit of one who tries to make the best of a very bad deal.

The position of the chiefs in the homelands is extremely difficult, and inherently false. Traditionally they were subject to strict controls by their own tribesmen, with whom they had to consult at every stage and who could either depose them if they were very unsatisfactory, or simply leave their area and join that of another chief of their choice. Such limited powers as they had, had steadily declined with the change in South

African society over the years and the immigration of so many Africans to the cities, so that eventually the chiefs retained only some ceremonial and ritual functions and a certain amount of nostalgic prestige.

The government, however, wishing to use them in administering and enforcing its separate development policies, has resurrected them, on the one hand arming them with powers which they never had before and on the other hand making them paid servants of the state, so that while they need not respond to the wishes of their people they must dance to the tune of the Government. The huts which one has seen burning in Pondoland and elsewhere were those of such Government-appointed chiefs and their supporters.

They control such vital matters as the grant of pensions, land and official jobs in their areas, and can also banish people and demolish their homes, without any of the traditional constraints operating on them. But if they do actively resist government policy, as numbers of them have done, they can be sacked from office and banished to a remote area.

Chief Gatsha Buthelezi of the Zulus was among those who held out longest against it but eventually announced, in April 1970, that the economic price of opposing the Bantustan policy was too high and said that the Zulus would try it 'as an experiment', though with very serious reservations. Nor did he have any illusions about the real bargaining position of the blacks in the situation: 'each and every one of you knows that as blacks we operate from a position of powerlessness,' he said.

At their most extreme the opponents of the homelands would argue that the entire project is window-dressing, merely there to give a concrete basis to the policy of the forced removal of black population groups. That these are places where their 'surplus appendages' – a classic white South African description of black peoples' families – may be sent when not needed in the work force of the white areas, where black political energies may be absorbed in internal political activity in their own tribal areas, and where pockets of intensive agriculture and cottage industry development may be concentrated in selected areas to demonstrate to overseas visitors and others the evidence of the great progress being made by South Africa in leading her black people to peaceful prosperity.

The land area allocated to the black people of the country for their homelands is about 13 per cent of the total area, split into numerous fragments. Buthelezi refers to them contemptuously as 'polka dots', because of their scattered appearance on the map of South Africa. 'It is ridiculous to say we can be a nation of polka dots,' he said. Nor is he interested in merely seeing Zululand's 29 pieces being somehow joined up into a unit, but he and several other homeland leaders want to see all the African areas joined up into a whole new African country, if there is going to be any real separate development. 'The Government has committed us to eight federal nations through this polka dot arrangement,' said Buthelezi at a seminar organised by the California Institute of Technology in 1972, 'but if they want to make a nation of us then we must consolidate into a single African bloc.' This is, of course, totally at variance with official government policy on the matter.

It is sometimes argued that the 13 per cent of the country set aside for 75 per cent of its population is in fact in the best rainfall area of the country, and it is true that most of it does lie in the eastern half of the country which gets reasonable rain rather than in the extensive desert and semi-desert areas to the west (most of South Africa is dry, arid, eroded 'badland'). But a great deal of the reserves lie in very hilly country, eroded and impoverished through over-crowding and over-stocking and frequent grass-burning to bring on the early grazing, the ecology disastrously damaged by people constantly cutting trees and bushes down for firewood. Hills like those of the Transkei and Natal's Valley of a Thousand Hills are delightfully scenic but very hard to farm, as any hill farmer living on a subsidy in Wales or Scotland will tell you. The University of Natal's Institue for Social Research said of Zululand: 'If the factor of excessive slope and low rainfall alone are considered, about 70 per cent of the areas of the Bantu reserves can be regarded as land of poor quality and generally unsuited to cultivation.'

People have been crowded and compressed into these 'native reserves,' as they used to be called, and homelands as their new official name describes them, until they have reached the highest population densities in the continent of Africa. In Kenya, for example, which is seriously worried about its own population explosion, the average population density is 41 per square mile, somewhat higher than the average for the whole continent. But the average population density of the homelands was 119 per square mile in 1970, ranging between 61 per square mile in the arid Bophutatswana homeland to 173 per square mile in Kwazulu. In white South Africa the average density of the total population, all races included, is only 35 per square mile, although all the big cities lie in the white areas.

At the same time there is a steady growth of the population of Blacks in the white urban areas, and it has proceeded throughout this century at a much faster rate than that of the white population. Between 1911 and 1960, according to South African official statistics, the total urban population increased over 2.8 times, while the urban African population increased over seven times. The proportion of Africans living in the urban areas was 12 per cent in 1921 and 30 per cent by 1970, by which time more than half of the total black population of South Africa was living in white areas. There is constant pressure under a variety of acts, regulations and control systems to regulate this population, both to control its absolute numbers present in white areas and to change its composition from families to single male migrant workers. For years now there have been constant deportations of old people, women and children as 'redundant Bantu' to their homelands, though some of them may be the third generation of a family born and brought up in a so-called white area, with no agricultural background and no real ties in the homeland which they have never seen until forcibly endorsed out and made to go there.

The South Africans expect to have a population of 50 million by the end of this century, and on present trends 90 per cent of them will live in towns and cities. White South Africans see it as increasingly urgent that they should move as many as possible of the Blacks in this fast-growing population into their respective homelands and locate all their political rights and aspirations there as well, or else they see themselves as being engulfed in a great tidal wave of black humanity.

On the economic prospects for these homelands, numerous studies by South African economists of all political persuasions, as well as by outsiders, show that the homelands have got very little chance of ever becoming economically viable. Government politicians are obliged to say in public, from time to time, that they are determined to make the homelands economically viable to emphasise how much work and money is being devoted to this end but in private conversations in Pretoria the top men express concern as to the likelihood of this ever coming about.

But it is not cynicism which causes the government of South Africa to produce a few concentrated showpiece areas rather than to raise the entire areas of the homelands to a uniform standard of advanced farming practice and full employment – it is simply that the scale of such an enterprise would be vastly beyond the capacity of the country to undertake. Allister Sparks of the *Rand Daily Mail* commented after going on a tour of inspection of the impressive irrigation scheme based on the Qamata Dam in the Transkei: 'It is a wonderful achievement by a band of dedicated officials. But it does not have much importance when set against the reality of South Africa's population explosion.'

Some would argue, of course, that what is spent on the homelands is derisory in comparison to what is spent on the white areas, or indeed most other sectors. Barbara Rogers, in a report prepared for International Defence and Aid, comments: 'Compared with a total of R73 million spent on the Bantustans in 1970, a mere 2.8 per cent of current government expenditure, R404 million was spent on security in 1969-1970, including police, prisons, the army and secret police . . . of all investments in public projects, only about 6 per cent are flowing into the Bantustans, and a negligible proportion of private capital.' At the same time, however, right wing white voters often attack their government for spending too much on the black areas.

Great globular figures of millions are boring and can easily be twisted to make contradictory points but to get some idea of the scale of the problem we should look at a few basic facts: the reserves or homelands have always been dependent on sources of income in the white economy and this trend is steadily increasing. In 1960-61 the ratio of domestic income from migrant workers was 47:53. Only six years later, by 1966-67, this had become 42:58. The best manpower from the homelands is constantly, and increasingly, being creamed off by employers in the white areas and all that comes back to the homelands from these workers is that portion of their earnings which they are able to save and remit home to their 'surplus appendages'. No multiplier effect, therefore, in the homelands from the spending of the main portion of their earning, which takes place in the white areas where they work.

There is no real prospect of any large-scale industry developing in the homelands in the foreseeable future. Industry goes where the factors of production and marketing are most favourable, in or near the established large urban complexes in the white areas, not to remote hillsides with no facilities for skilled staff and their families, no real communications networks and no market. The authorities have tried inducements and pressure to get industrialists to establish factories on the borders of homelands or inside them but with extremely limited success. South African economists, whether English or Afrikaans-speaking and whether they support Government policy or not, tend to be hard-headed professionals and many of the most damning studies of the economic trends and prospects of the homelands have come from Afrikaner economists and their unfavourable comments can hardly be a question of taking sides for political reasons. Mr C. J. Human told the annual congress of the Afrikaner businessmens' institute (Afrikaanse Handels Instituut) that the number of job opportunities created for Africans in the decentralised areas (which include areas not necessarily in the homelands themselves but generally contiguous to them) was 68,500 in the decade 1960-70. 'If this figure is compared with the economically-active non-white population of almost six million we can see how far we still have to go', he said.

Professor H. J. Reynders, who was at that time with Pretoria University and subsequently became head of the Federated Chamber of Industries, estimated that for border industry around the homelands to absorb the new labour coming from them, would require a further 40,000 jobs a year until 1980, and 53,000 from then until 1990. But according to a study by Mr P. J. Reynolds, from 1960 to 1969 an extra expenditure of R314 million had produced jobs for only 54,000 Africans in these areas – a job creation rate about seven times too little for the estimated requirements.

According to official figures of the Department of the Interior, the Transkei – which is by no means the worst area – had a labour force of 250,000 active males available for wage employment, not including 105,000 working on the land, mostly in subsistence farming. Of these, 41,000, or 1/ of the total, were employed in the Transkei, mainly in government, commerce or domestic service. Another 155,400 were away temporarily as migrant workers, mainly in the gold mines. This leaves about 64,000 unemployed – an unemployment rate of around 25 per cent.

That is a rate of unemployment which the Western world remembers as the worst economic nightmare of this century – The Great Depression of the 1930's – but the people of the South African homelands have to live with it all the time. They do not get the dole and those of them who are lucky enough to get work on average one-sixth of what white people earn in South Africa.

13 For the Specialist

With their great liking for order, progress and the benefits of prosperity, South Africans have built up a general network of industrial and urban facilities which would do credit to a bigger country with more skills to draw on. In a certain sense they have made a highly rational use of the division of labour principle, the Blacks being on the whole available to do the simpler tasks, leaving the Whites with time to concentrate on the more complex ones. In certain fields, such as mining, water conservation and the handling of the African environment in its broadest sense, they are among the world leaders. They tend to pick out certain projects which they think will be of the greatest benefit and then to give them their head, allocating resources and money to such favoured projects with a generosity and imagination which must often be the envy of other countries. It is a society, also, in which expertise and proficiency are much admired – there is great respect for the man who is good at his job.

Take the South African Bureau of Standards (SABS) for example. It has been developed to the point where it is said that there is only one other in the world which has such an extensive range of abilities – and that belongs to Russia. The South African Bureau grew for the best possible reasons – because the country clearly needed it. At the time South Africa struck gold, late last century, its industry was well behind that of Europe and America. Machinery in great quantities and from all parts of the industrial world started arriving virtually overnight, there was no standardisation and for a time there was chaos. The Transvaal Chamber of Mines made the first effort to sort matters out with a standardisation committee in 1905, which was followed by other similar committees until eventually the Bureau of Standards was set up in 1945. So the new Bureau had some history, experience and expertise to build on. Its function was to prepare national standards and codes of practice and to provide information and aid in matters of standardisation. It has built up a reputation for reliable standards and sound information so considerable that several African states who have been on terms of enmity, politically, with South Africa for years, nevertheless would not dream of trusting anybody else to check and pass all sorts of vital equipment on which their economies depend, such as mining.

The Bureau today is housed in a multi-million rand complex in Pretoria, quite close to the centre of the city. In its 55 laboratories and testing rooms the equipment ranges from small quaint contrivances improvised from bicycle-chains and gear-wheels through bizarre facilities such as a room containing four million live cockroaches to a great sealed shock-proof steel chamber housing the Bureau's most delicate high-precision instruments and hangar-like structures – one of them containing a 3.2 million volt 'impulse generator' which can produce man-made lightning in bolts several yards long. Situated at a discreet distance from the main complex is a particularly solidly-built little building without many external windows in which the Bureau tests explosives and highly inflammable materials.

It has a staff of 1000, some of them qualified to professorial level. It has, to date, published well over 1000 standard specifications and codes of practice and more than 600 test methods, and more than 1000 private purchasing specifications for outside organizations, as well as hundreds of specifications for state departments and local authorities.

In manufactured goods, it aims at standards nothing short of excellent, which it keeps up through a system of SABS standardisation marks – hard to earn, the products which bear them regularly checked by the Bureau for uniform quality control, but a great asset to both the manufacturer in defining the quality of his goods or services, and the consumer. The annual sale of products bearing the coveted SABS marks is well over R300 million a year in South Africa alone, and the country has of course a steadily expanding export market not only for primary and agricultural products and semi-processed materials, but also for sophisticated manufactured goods; (it is, to take a random example, the main supplier to the United States of replacement exhaust systems for imported motor cars.)

The SABS is a founder member of the International Organisation for Standardisation and represented on associated international bodies. It has also spread its wings in recent years and formed a Design Institute to promote better design in South African products, and a National Productivity Institute to encourage productivity 'in every sphere.' The Bureau has also been in charge of the massive programme for changing over to the metric system. Bodies like the Design Institute tend to be effectively staffed, well-run and prestigious in South Africa, especially if officially recognised or sponsored.

When institutions are favoured by governments and given everything they want to achieve the highest standards, it makes for high morale and a good spirit among the workers there. It is pleasant to recall the special table of white-haired old gentlemen that I saw at one of the SABS annual occasions, who were not only invited along but given a place of honour and made to feel especially welcome, their former days spent working for the Bureau remembered and appreciated by their young successors. One may take the SABS as typical of the more progressive State-backed organisations in South Africa.

Also near to Pretoria is the famous Onderstepoort Veterinary Research Institute, whose vaccines have been responsible for protecting millions of head of stock not only in South Africa but in many other African countries as well. They produce 100 million doses a year there. Problems of parasites, animal diseases, and climatic conditions, are of course common to many countries, so that the work at Onderstepoort is vitally important to people so far afield that some of them have scarcely heard of South Africa, though they do know that the areas they are living in and farming were closed by animal and human disease to their grandfathers. Outside Africa, vaccines from Onderstepoort are called for by Australia, South America, Hong Kong, New Zealand, Iran, St Helena and the United States.

There is a very wide range of research institutions in South Africa, of a scale and quality which one would expect from a much bigger, more fully industrialised country. South Africans like to refer to it sometimes as 'the workshop of Africa' and it is clearly in the best position to be that workshop – or perhaps better still, laboratory – than any other country south of the Sahara.

The most high-powered centralized institution for research is the Council for Scientific and Industrial Research (CSIR), which also lives in a superbly-equipped complex of buildings outside Pretoria, in landscaped, meticulously-gardened grounds entered through a rather futuristic system of electrically-controlled gates. The CSIR, in turn, runs a National Institute for Water Research, among many other ambitious enterprises, which has done advanced work on recycling water used for sewage – South Africa is short of only two vital commodities, oil (non-existent) and water (scarce). The CSIR attracts some of the top scientific brains in the country and appears to provide them with good pay, excellent working conditions and challenging assignments, but one must register one objection – it is exceedingly difficult for professional writers to find out what they are doing and to report on it; the CSIR insists on an amazingly complex and cumbersome system of checking back everything that is written about them. Apart from the usual South African obsession with secrecy, security and discretion they do of course have some real reasons for being cautious about their information, since they are often engaged in industrial research on behalf of commercial organisations which could be ruined if certain information found its way into the hands of their competitors.

There is also a Human Sciences Research Council and the

South African Medical Research Council (South Africans believe confidently that they have the best doctors in the world, which would be difficult to prove or disprove, but Professor Barnard doing the world's first successful heart transplant has done nothing to diminish this belief). There is an Atomic Energy Board, with a gigantic nuclear plant doing research on reactor fuels – and who knows what else – behind its barbed-wire security fences among the Magakesberg mountains.

There is a National Institute for Metallurgy, a Department of Agricultural Technical Services, a Geological Survey run by the Department of Mines and numerous technical bodies organised and financed by particular industries or professions, such as the South African Institute of Civil Engineers. The latter even provides a free technical advisory service to neighbouring Lesotho and recently advised Lesotho on its new international airport and a major road. There is also a National Institute for Road Research.

Government departments such as Posts and Telegraphs, Health and Community Development are also great repositories of expertise, very often used by neighbouring states and usually functioning at a level of competence which, by international standards, ranges from sound to excellent. There are also 16 universities equipped for research and there are about 40 important private industrial laboratories and, of course, numerous smaller ones.

South Africans may justifiably enjoy their pride in the achievements of their scientists and research workers, whose numbers are disproportionately high in relation to the number of the population educated in the Western technological system. It was Professor C. Smith, South Africa's 'fish man' who discovered the coelocanth living fossil, which had been believed extinct many millions of years ago. Christian Persoon was one of the first scientists to study fungi and is today known as the father of mycology, Dr. Y. Atherstone, of little Grahamstown, was successfully using ether within a few months of the first Americans trying it out as an anaesthetic. Raymond Dart's discoveries produced examples of the earliest of man's ape-like ancestors. Alex du Toit was one of the first geologists to develop the theory of continental drift, now becoming widely accepted. Robert Broom opened up the veritable fossil mines of the Karroo to the world, and South African scientists have played a respectable part in the geological search for the 'missing contintent' of Gondwanaland indicated by this theory.

In recent years opposition to the the political system in their native land has led to a considerable 'brain drain' of highly qualified South Africans and they are now to be met throughout the English-speaking world, where South African self-confidence stands them in good stead and they very frequently occupy high positions in commerce, industry or the professions. Many of them are on the faculties of leading universities in the United Kingdom and the USA. It is ironic that several of the most outspoken former South African leftists have made fortunes speculating in property in London. Early training will take you a long way.

The country is shaped, they always say, like a tortoise's back, so that the rather sparse amount of water which does fall in it tends to run off rapidly, scouring precious topsoil away with it. In recent years South Africa has made strenuous efforts to counteract this disadvantage, with generous grants for farmers to make a variety of conservation dams and with some truly gargantuan state river-taming projects in which water is dammed on a major river, to be piped and channeled many hundreds of miles away to where it is needed most.

Industry, one sometimes forgets, uses even more water than agriculture, so for a country that has to run fast to stay in the same place, because of its rapid population growth, it is essential that this vital resource be handled as effectively as possible. Appropriately enough, therefore, the country's greatest civil engineering project is a dam and a distribution system to harness the Orange River – one of the country's two biggest watercourses. About 60 per cent of the country gets less than 20 inches of rain a year, and most of the water from the country's largest river, the Orange, flows into the sea. This problem has for long been the subject of much thought and planning and eventually work began in 1962 on a £200 million pound project. The dam, just completed, has a shoreline of 250 miles, with many islands, making a man-made lake, 144 square miles in extent. The six radial gates of the dam wall for controlling the floodwater, contain 95 tons of moving parts each and have a life expectancy of three centuries: when led through tunnels and channels to the Fish River valley and the Sundays River the new water available for irrigation will make it possible to establish 9,000 new farms; it will benefit six major towns and numerous small towns over an area extending for more than 500 miles in radius.

South Africa is often called a very rich country, and in terms of natural resources it is certainly rich, but it is very arguable whether any country in which three-quarters of the people are poor, can be called rich. Certainly, it looks rich, with its wealthy white suburbs, great marshalling yards to be seen from the air, and industrial areas which generally look refreshingly clean and new compared to, say, the Midlands of Britain, creating an impression of modernity and efficiency.

One might say that the cash economy, the Western sector, is well developed and that those who are allowed to participate in it fully are rich, comparatively speaking, but even in pure economic terms the question of racial policy is all-important. Put very briefly, what the problem amounts to is that the South African economy is essentially an expanding one, and has to remain that way for the foreseeable future if for no other reason than that the population is also expanding rapidly. Production of goods and services therefore has to expand to keep pace and this means that the skilled manpower has to be available to produce the goods, and has to earn the money to buy them as well. But the racial and cultural differences between the major part of the workforce, the black people, and the major providers of capital and management, the Whites, splits them apart and prevents the economy from developing naturally. The policy of keeping the races apart cuts right across the natural tendency of the economy's growth, which is to pull them together physically in close proximity, since you cannot very well have a factory with its management living and working in Johannesburg and its workers working and living in Zululand.

The Federated Chamber of Industries – which represents simply industry, and no particular viewpoint or political party – argues constantly with Government departments who try to enforce, for example, predetermined ratios of white to black workers in certain areas and certain industries. The government is by no means unsympathetic to these arguments and relations are good between F.C.i. economic analysts, tariff experts and their opposite numbers in the government institutions. But the government does have to appease its white voters and also wrestle with the intractable problem of regulating the numbers of population groups in different areas. Without getting involved in the politics of the issue the latter is a problem which is known throughout Africa – the great pull of the few glittering cities as opposed to the relatively poor and uneventful tribal existence. The South African Reserve Bank also has to wrestle, but in this case not with people but with an economy which suddenly goes into a steep dive and resists all efforts to pull it out, then just as suddenly over-reacts in the other direction and tries to roar upwards. Nobody could be better suited temporarily to the potentially hair-raising job of working the main controlling levers of this vigorously self-willed economy than the unflappable gentlemen of the South African Reserve Bank in Pretoria. The bank recruits them from among the most brilliant young economists as soon as it spots them in the universities. These men have come to occupy a highly-respected place, not only in formulating and administering financial policy in South Africa, but in the role they play as controllers of the world's largest source of newly-mined gold, and in the work of international bodies trying to regulate world financial fluctuations, like the International Monetary Fund. This is no denigration of the equally important work of the permanent officials of the Treasury, but they work under the handicap of having, from time to time, new political masters who do not necessarily share their expertise but insist on sharing their work.

When it reaches the bottom of one of its periodic troughs the South African economy tends to suffer from 'stagflation', a particularly unnerving state in which although the economy is stagnant in terms of producing extra goods, prices keep on climbing. New money continues to come in from overseas and a great deal of it seems to find its way into financing the import of manufactured goods from overseas as well. Businessmen having dealings with South Africa will therefore find that although it is theoretically a completely free, open, capitalistic system, it also has a great apparatus of controls to try and regulate these tendencies – price controls, import controls, ceilings on commercial bank credit ratios, controls on hire-purchase and altogether a highly-developed system of fiscal, monetary and direct controls designed to help them steer that awkward economy along a safe course.

Nor will South Africa allow 'hot money' to come pouring into the country during times of international currency upheaval. The last thing they want to see is thousands of millions of pounds, dollars, francs, marks and yen pouring in, seeking a safe haven and a quick return, pushing South African land prices, for example, out of the reach of South Africans, and then just as suddenly pouring out again, leaving a disastrous depression. Not that such attempts are not made: 'we get so many people trying to push the wrong kind of money in here that we practically have to beat them off with sticks', said one staid Pretoria mandarin of money.

What they do like is money for investment in state projects or industry, which generally offers investors a good return. Americans, for example, earn an average 15 percent on the 500 million dollars they have in South Africa, and the United Kingdom – South Africa's biggest backer – gets an average 11.5 per cent on its £1,500 million in South Africa. (This is about three times greater than the average on all its other international investments).

The prospects for future economic development are really very good. It is usual to make the proviso that because of the racial tension anything can happen, but in fact there is a growing black middle class which must act as a living example of the benefits which material prosperity can confer. At the same time there is a growing official acceptance of industry's argument that in the long run everybody will be better off if blacks are allowed to be trained for skilled jobs and then properly paid for doing them. So that however the South Africans work out the problems of intergrating of disintegrating their racially diverse society, they have a vast reservoir of manpower and purchasing power of which they have really only begun to tap the edges, together with natural resources enough to make them all rich.

They have a well-developed financial system – sophisticated banking houses equal to anything in the Western world, a lively stock exchange (positively frenetic, at times) and a highly developed capital market. The pattern is changing in a healthy way fron a purely extractive form of industry to a manufacturing form and agriculture is becoming more intensive and more productive. In the period 1962 to 1968, for example, the country's dependence on agriculture as a producer of its wealth, declined from 12 per cent to 10 per cent and mining went down from 14 per cent to 12 per cent in the same period, while the contribution of manufacturing industry rose from 19 per cent to 21 per cent. Industrial products themselves were at first largely centred on mining and the railway system towards the end of the last century. Then they developed, particularly during World War Two, to a phase of import substitution protected at critical points by tariffs and now they are moving well into the next, much more advanced phase, of manufacturing in response to the growth of special demands and export requirements.

The great attraction for foreign investors in South Africa in former years was cheap labour. Those days, if not quite gone, are certainly on the way out and any prospective employer would be ill-advised to try and make his fortune in South Africa on that basis now. It was instructive to watch the government reaction in Pretoria in 1971, when there were widespread strikes in the textile industry against wages which had not been increased in some cases, for 14 years. Africans are not allowed to organize themselves into trade unions and strike action by them is illegal. However the authorities confined themselves to preventing the picketing becoming violent and protecting the plants which were being picketed, and did not take any intimidatory action against the black strikers, though legally they could have prosecuted them. One of the employers concerned, who had built himself up a very large personal fortune in the last two decades but continued to pay his workers wages below the 'poverty datum line', arrived in Pretoria to protest that he was not being given official backing to force his workers to give up their strike. He was told quite bluntly, one learned in the corridors of the Union Buildings, 'you have had a very good innings – now it's time you started paying them a decent wage.'

And of course, as the government's economic advisers are well aware, although paying those workers a decent wage might initially mean that their employer might have to give up one of his two private aeroplanes, the extra spending power they earn will generate wealth for a great many other people in the country, as well as greatly improving the lot of the employees themselves.

The country's minerals remain an exciting prospect for further development. The future of gold, which contributed most to South Africa's wealth, is now less bright both in terms of the open market price for the metal as the world monetary bodies work increasingly to free currencies from gold, and also in terms of the life-span of the South African mine-fields, which do not seem likely to last out the century. But there are numerous other minerals still waiting or in an early stage of exploitation. The country is the world's biggest producer of platinum and electrolytic copper, ferro-chrome and ferro-manganese. It shares the top position as world's biggest producer of antimony, chrome, lithium and manganese; it is the third largest producer of uranium, asbestos and vanadium, it is well up in nickel production and has healthy supplies of many other minerals including plentiful coal.

Although it has only six per cent of the total population of Africa its production output is equal to that of one quarter of the whole continent. The state apparatus for controlling and regulating all this activity has been growing steadily in recent years and one can see this in economic terms when one observes that the proportion of public sector contributions to total domestic investment went up from 40 per cent a year at the beginning of the 1960s, to 50 per cent by the time the seventies arrived. There are frequent rumblings about a 'growing army of bureaucrats', and the activities of the state's Industrial Development Corporation are closely watched by the private sector, to see that it does not exceed its brief of acting as an agent of development and helping promising sectors of industry through their infancy. The state has for some time run the railway systems, harbours and airways, the South African Iron and Steel Corporation, the Electricity Supply Commision, the South African Coal, Oil and Gas Corporation and, of course, the South African Broadcasting Corporation.

Nevertheless, the position appears still to be reasonably balanced between state control and private development, and overseas investors appear to find it satisfactory enough: 74 per cent of total foreign investment in South Africa is invested in the private sector.

All that remains, as Chief Luthuli once put it, is to give all the people of South Africa a fair share in the land of their birth.

Index